EDUCATION

Other books by Gordon Bietz

Seventh-day Adventist Higher Education in North America
(coauthored with Steve Pawluk)

EDUCATION
Gordon Bietz

Pacific Press®
Publishing Association
Nampa, Idaho | www.pacificpress.com

Additional copies of this book are available for purchase by calling toll-free 1-800-765-6955 or by visiting adventistbookcenter.com.

ISBN: 978-0-8163-6589-0

July 2020

Contents

Preface

You will find at the end of some chapters in this book a story set in the mythical place called Fenton Forest. During my thirteen years as the pastor of the Southern Adventist University Church in Collegedale, Tennessee, I found that concluding my sermons with a story that summarized the point of the sermon engaged adult and child alike. I hope these stories provide a way for children to understand the chapter's point and for adults to remember it as well.

I want to acknowledge the members of the Southern Adventist University church and the students from kindergarten through university who encouraged me through their comments and participation in services. Most of all, I am grateful to my family, Cynthia, Gina, and Julie, who patiently listened to those Fenton Forest stories and made many suggestions.[1]

The Latin origin of the word *education* means "to nourish." Just as we need daily physical food, we need to be regularly nourished spiritually. Christian education is spiritual nourishment for the mind, and teachers can present challenging thoughts that awaken deeper spiritual commitment among the students. Sabbath School professors fulfill their teaching responsibility by occasionally creating an incongruity that compels students to think about how to resolve it. To this end, you can use a Fenton Forest story, asking the class about the moral it communicates.

Additionally, teachers need to create an inclusive environment in which class members feel free to participate in the discussion. One way to do that is to use some of the stories and illustrations in this book as discussion starters.

For example, in chapter 1, I relate the story of how my grandfather moved his house to be close to the church so that his children could have a Christian education. Questions that might be asked include:

- Is that reasonable today?
- How can we emphasize the importance of Christian education in our cultural context?
- Do we find that same level of commitment to nourishing our young people in Christian life today?
- How is a high level of commitment to Christian education manifested today?

Teaching Sabbath School is a high and holy calling. In this book, I have endeavored to help you answer the call in a way that edifies God and His church. As you think about the illustrations and stories in these pages, consider their potential to spark discussion and nourish the spirit of our Seventh-day Adventist families.

---

1. Some have expressed concern about telling fictional stories in which animals talk. I would refer those who have doubts about using fiction to Judges 9:7–15, where Jotham used a story with trees talking, and to the fictional story Jesus told about the rich man and Lazarus in Luke 16:19–31.

One

Education in the Garden of Eden

My grandfather emigrated from a German settlement in Ukraine in the late nineteenth century. In his early years in the United States, he could read little English. One year at camp meeting, he bought a book by Ellen White that had been translated into German. It contained a statement saying, "It is no longer safe to send them [our children] to the public school."[1] This statement created a problem for my grandparents.

They had homesteaded in Kidder County, North Dakota, and had built a two-story house on the land. The problem was that the house was several miles from the nearest Adventist church, over in Bowden County, too far for his nine children to take the horse and buggy to school every day. So my grandparents determined to move. They purchased a quarter section (160 acres) of land just one mile from the church. But this created another problem.

There was no house on the new property since it was just farmland, so my grandfather decided to move the house he had built. He hired two steam-propelled engines used for harvesting, attached them to the house, and over the next three days, pulled the house to the new property close to the church.

At first, there was not even a school in operation at the church. But my grandfather's commitment to a Christian education caught on, and before long, Bowdon County Church School was opened at the church.

My uncle Emil fondly remembered that as long as the Bietz children were in the elementary grades, a church school was in operation. He quoted my grandfather as saying, "If none of the other members send their children to church school, mine will be there. We'll always have a school, even if I have to board the teacher and pay the salary."[2] One year my grandparents did just that.

The value of Christian education

Public schools in the late 1800s—especially in a rural North Dakota agrarian community—did not face the influences of television, internet, and smartphones, yet my grandparents resolved that Christian education was a priority. They had a "Garden of Eden" vision for an environment in which their children would find their identity in Jesus among peers in a Christian community.

My father maintained that same priority for my brother and me. As kids, we were driven many miles to attend a Christian school when the excellent public schools in our district would have been much more convenient for my parents. It was in that school that I crystalized my commitment to Jesus and gave my life to Him. It was there among the influence of my peers and mentors that I slowly made the transition from "my parents' religion" to personally choosing my faith for myself.

Even if I had not been the church pastor when our daughters were school age, there would not have been a question about where my wife and I wanted to send them. The public and prep schools in our area were known for excellent teachers and high academic quality, but we also wanted our daughters to have an environment under the influence of friends and teachers from the church. They received excellent academic training and are professionally successful today, but more important, these days, I find I am learning about spirituality from them.

As Ellen White says in the book *Education*, "True education means more than the perusal of a certain course of study. It means more than a preparation for the life that now is. It has to do with the whole being, and with the whole period of existence possible to man. It is the harmonious development of the physical, the mental, and the spiritual powers. It prepares the student for the joy of service in this world and for the higher joy of wider service in the world to come."[3]

Education is about life itself, getting to know the Creator of life. In the Garden of Eden, getting to know the Creator was walking with God "in the cool of the day" (Genesis 3:8, KJV). In the imperfect secular environment of our world, getting to know the Creator is walking with mentors and peers who believe in their Creator. It is in a living learning community where they will walk with Jesus.

The dangers of society

Some would suggest that integrating young people into society by exposing them to the world works like a vaccine. They believe exposing young people to the world and its temptations inoculates them against those temptations, similar to the way the body develops immunity through controlled exposure to a disease. Some proponents of this theory express concern that Christian schools are too much like incubators, isolating the young from the world.

In today's digital world, it would be impossible to isolate young people even if we wanted to. What they need is to be surrounded by mentors and peers of faith so that they can experience life in a community of faith without being immersed in the world. The goal is to provide an environment where the world can be seen from the Christian point of view. This type of "incubator," or garden, provides the necessary environment for growth so that students, when confronted by the world, can handle the challenges to their faith.

Henry Dunster, the first president of Harvard, stated that every student should "be plainly instructed and earnestly pressed to consider well [that] the main end of his life and studies is to know God and Jesus Christ which is eternal life."[4] That was the original goal of most schools established on Christian principles, but as James Burtchaell points out in his book *The Dying of the Light: The Disengagement of Colleges and Universities From Their Christian Churches*, most of those schools no longer stand by those principles. Most universities and colleges have moved from the belief of their founders to the disbelief of secular culture.

One need not reflect for long on the public-school environment or the secular college/university environment of agnosticism and atheism to understand that it is not conducive to finding God's answers to life's most profound questions. Public higher education today has traveled a long way from the Garden of Eden.

In the Garden of Eden, arguably a perfect environment, Satan managed to confront our original parents with the lie that if they partook of the fruit of the tree of the knowledge of good and evil, they not only would never die but would be like God.[5]

So even in a perfect environment, Adam and Eve exercised their God-given gift of free will to disobey him. Today, our world is full of proverbial trees of knowledge of good and evil. Satan has many avenues for confronting students with schemes that would derail God's plan for their lives. Adventist Christian schools are not Garden-of-Eden perfect, but the chance for mentors and friends to positively influence spiritual growth is much better than at any secular public school or university.

Arthur F. Holmes, former professor of Christian philosophy at Wheaton College, puts it another way. "We need to ask how values are transmitted. Young people assimilate them more from example than precept, more from their peers than from their elders, and more by being involved than by being spectators."[6]

In a Christian setting, the peer group—the community of students that come together in a living learning community—creates the environment for the maturing of faith. In such a setting, they can be involved in Christian service rather than just being spectators on Sabbath. It is as students connect in a faith environment that they develop the character to be counterculture Christians resisting the secular culture. The apostle John offers this cautionary note: "Don't love the world's ways. Don't love the world's goods. Love of the world squeezes out love for the Father. Practically everything that goes on in the world—wanting your own way, wanting everything for yourself, wanting to appear important—has nothing to do with the Father. It just isolates you from him. The world and all its wanting, wanting, wanting is on the way out—but whoever does what God wants is set for eternity" (1 John 2:15–17, *The Message*).

Or as Ellen White put it, "To love Him, the infinite, the omniscient One, with the whole strength, and mind, and heart, means the highest development of every power. It means that in the whole being—the body, the mind, as well as the soul—the image of God is to be restored."[7]

In the Garden of Eden, Satan directly contradicted God

when he claimed Adam and Eve would not die but would become like God (Genesis 3:4, 5). His lie is reminiscent of Isaiah's description of Lucifer seeking to be like God (Isaiah 14:12–14). The temptation many have today is to go to Ivy League schools or private, expensive high schools, where some believe the young people will get smarter and get careers that could make them, if not like gods, at least like the rich and famous. As Ellen White put it, "By every species of deception, he [Satan] is endeavoring to induce man to eat of the forbidden tree. He thus tempts man to disobedience by leading him to believe that he is entering a wonderful field of knowledge. But this is all a deception. Elated with his ideas of progression, man is setting his feet in the path that leads to degradation and death. Satan, in a deceptive garb, still lurks in the tree of knowledge."[8]

Eve was deceived when she saw that the fruit on the tree looked good. It was physically appealing to her, as there are things about an Ivy League education that appeal. John Milton, in the epic poem *Paradise Lost*, expresses the appeal of the forbidden fruit in the mouth of Eve:

> Here grows the Cure of all, this Fruit Divine,
> Fair to the Eye, inviting to the Taste,
> Of vertue to make wise: what hinders then
> To reach, and feed at once both Bodie and Mind?[9]

"The cure of all" is the exclusivity of being one of the few accepted, the knowledge that you are above average, the appeal of bragging about your educational understanding—all these attract the human side of selfishness, the desire to be the smartest person in the room, to attend the most prestigious schools, to be exalted over those around you. Jesus, being God, humbled Himself, becoming nothing, to the point of death on the cross (Philippians 2:5–8). Paul appeals to us to behave in the same way (verses 3–5), yet the pursuit of educational attainment in a public institution can be about domination and power as contrasted with servanthood and self-denial. Ellen White describes the best school: "The system of education instituted at the beginning of the world was to be a model for man throughout all aftertime. As an illustration of its principles a model school was established in Eden, the home of our first parents. The Garden of Eden was the schoolroom, nature was the lesson book, the Creator Himself was the instructor, and the parents of the human family were the students."[10]

The goal of Christian education

The choice of schools depends on the goal of the education. If the goal is to follow Jesus and to serve humanity, learning at the feet of people who know Jesus provides the best training. Peter speaks of the world we face today: "Most importantly, I want to remind you that in the last days scoffers will come, mocking the truth and following their own desires. They will say, 'What happened to the promise that Jesus is coming again? From before the times of our ancestors, everything has remained the same since the world was first created' " (2 Peter 3:3, 4, NLT).

The goal of Christian education is found in Proverbs: "The fear of the LORD is the beginning of wisdom: and the knowledge of the holy is understanding" (Proverbs 9:10, KJV).

There never was a question in my grandparents' minds whether their nine children should have the benefit of a church school. They planned for it and believed in it, and the Lord saw them through their commitment. It wasn't always easy, but they believed that "the education received in childhood and youth affects their entire business career in mature life, and their religious experience bears a corresponding stamp."[11]

The founding philosophy of my grandparents' "Happy Home Farm," as they called it, was that "to have your children enter the gates of the City of God as conquerors, they must be educated to fear God and keep His commandments in the present life."[12]

My grandparents did not end up with a large farm, a lot of land, or extra savings in the bank, but they never regretted the money, time, work, and many prayers offered on behalf of their nine children. Their whole aim in life was to see their children accept the Lord Jesus, join the remnant church, and use whatever talents God gave them to be of service in the home, the church, the community, and society at large.

Of the nine children, each of the four sisters married ministers, three of the five brothers became ministers, and all of them remained in the church. "Point your kids in the right direction—when they're old they won't be lost" (Proverbs 22:6, *The Message*).

Fenton Forest

And for the children and those young at heart, a story. There once was a school in Fenton Forest. In this school, all the inhabitants of the forest learned how to avoid the traps that were placed in the forest by hunters that lived in the big city some miles away. In this school, there were classes such as "Theories of Trap Placement," "Trap Design," and "Emergency Medicine" for those who were caught in traps.

Two students enrolled in the school were Freddy Fox and his cousin Sam. Now, they were about as different as day and night. There was a wonderful teacher in the school, and Freddy paid close attention in class. Sam, on the other hand, made fun of the teacher and didn't listen in class.

Sam passed the class by memorizing a few things he had to and managing to remember them long enough to recognize them on the test.

Freddy, on the other hand, knew the teacher had a lot of experience and wanted to learn all he could about traps from the teacher so that he would not get caught. He spent some time after class with the teacher, asking more questions about trap design and placement. He had heard of some careless foxes who had lost some toes in a trap, and he didn't want to lose his.

Both Freddy and his cousin Sam graduated from school. Graduation night, there were the typical parties and celebrations at the Nut Hut in Fenton Forest. However, there was a tragedy the night of graduation that proved that you could get all As in class and still flunk life. Today, Freddy is a prosperous businessman in East Fenton Forest running a den construction firm. Sam, on the other hand, is decorating the shoulders of a lady in the big city.

---

1. Ellen G. White, *Child Guidance* (Nashville, TN: Southern Publishing, 1954), 304.

2. Reinhold Bietz, *Happy Home Farm: An Expression of the Faith and Fun in a Christian Home* (Brushton, NY: Teach Services, 1994).

3. Ellen G. White, *Education* (Mountain View, CA: Pacific Press®, 1903), 13.

4. Lynne Cheney, *A Time for Freedom: What Happened When in America* (New York: Simon & Schuster, 2005), 15.

5. "But you must not eat from the tree of the knowledge of good and evil, for when you eat of it you will surely die" (Genesis 2:17).

6. Arthur F. Holmes, *The Idea of a Christian College*, rev. ed. (Grand Rapids, MI: Eerdmans, 1987), 82.

7. White, *Education*, 16.

8. Ellen G. White, "The Tree of Life and the Tree of Knowledge," *Daily Bulletin of the General Conference*, March 6, 1899, 158.

9. John Milton, *Paradise Lost*, bk. 9, lines 776–779.

10. White, *Education*, 20.

11. Ellen G. White, *Testimonies for the Church*, vol. 3 (Mountain View, CA: Pacific Press®, 1948), 148. Testimony 22, which this is from, was originally published in 1872.

12. White, *Child Guidance*, 298.

Two

The Family

"Welcome home!" The customs agent greeted me as I reentered the United States after spending my junior year at the Adventist University of France—Collonges. It had been an enjoyable experience, and I was a little surprised by the warm feeling those words evoked. There is something extraordinary about being home. As George Bernard Shaw is quoted as saying, "A happy family is but an earlier heaven."[1]

The importance of family

Home is where the heart is, according to the old expression, but I also suggest that home is where the mind grows. When we think of where education takes place, a schoolroom might typically come to mind, but the premier educational institution is the home. According to First Things First, a nonprofit organization specializing in healthy relationship skills, 90 percent of a child's physical brain develops by the age of five.[2] The National Research Council reports that while "it was once commonly thought that infants lack the ability to form complex ideas," studies have shown that "very young children are competent, active agents of their own."[3]

Education

Many people who recognize the importance of the family in education are a part of a homeschool movement. By the year 2016, in the United States, an estimated 3.4 million adults had the experience of homeschooling for at least one of their K–12 years. Those who did were homeschooled an average of seven years. Approximately 2.3 million students are homeschooled today, bringing the total to an estimated 5.7 million Americans who have experienced homeschooling.[4] As Ellen White said, "The system of education established in Eden centered in the family. Adam was 'the son of God' (Luke 3:38), and it was from their Father that the children of the Highest received instruction. Theirs, in the truest sense, was a family school."[5]

The family creates an environment for education to occur. It is in the family that the modeling of the parents is copied by the child.

Some children, however, choose to disobey and follow a path that their parents would not want for them. And some parents spend their lives speculating about what they might have done wrong because their children did not "turn out" as they had hoped. Adam and Eve had a perfect home and still made terrible choices. Similarly, Cain and Abel are assumed to have had a good home, but when the two brothers were confronted with the opportunity to honor God, their responses differed drastically.

How do we understand different responses to life? God has granted freedom of will to every human being, and Adam, Eve, and Cain demonstrated wills that were not aligned with God. You might say that while God provided the right education, they exercised free will and followed the counsel of Satan.

The power of approval

The Bible tells the story of a dysfunctional family in which the couple was childless for a time, but then they had twin boys. These twins were not at all identical. One was Daddy's boy, and the other was Mama's boy. Daddy's boy loved to play outside. He was a rough-and-tumble kid and stayed dirty most of the time. When he would track mud into the house, his mother complained, "Can't you clean your feet when you come into this house? Go wash your hands! Why can't you be more like your brother?"

Mama's boy, on the other hand, rarely tracked mud into the house. He was kind and considerate, sensitive to his mother's needs. Daddy didn't get along as well with him. Daddy liked to fish and hunt, but this kid didn't want to hurt the fish or kill the animals. He would get homesick when he was away from his mother for a few days.

With the mother approving one son and the father supporting the other, sibling rivalry was intense. It got so bad that one of the brothers ran away from home in fear that the other would kill him. Jacob and Esau were troubled children in a dysfunctional family. Neither brother had the approval of both parents.

From the start of life, we seek approval—whether we are two years old going down the slide and looking to our mother for approval or in elementary school playing kickball and seeking approval from our peers. Seeking affirmation from others is built into our minds—whether from schoolteachers or marriage partners.

Think back to the time you were in school. Which teachers had the most impact on your life? Was it the ones with the most knowledge about the subject or the ones who connected with you by showing an interest in you as a person? What is true for teachers in school is true of parents in the home. Expressing appreciation for young people builds a relationship with them that enables the adult to be an influence in the life of the young person.

Ryan was one of those incorrigible students who grew up in an abusive home, and in the fourth grade, his behavior was so challenging that he was banished to a class for delinquents. The first day in the new class, he hurled his desk at the teacher. But instead of throwing him out of class, she asked, "Is everything OK at home? Why are you so angry?" Elizabeth Hughes was an insightful teacher, and she saw that his behavior, although directed for the moment at her, had its origin in a dysfunctional family at home.

On another occasion, when Ryan was at home, he threatened his family by pulling out a knife. The police were called, and he was placed in juvenile detention. While there, the only supportive contact with the outside world came from Mrs. Hughes, who called him and said, "Don't let this define you. You can do better."[6] His caseworker also showed him love even as he cursed her. Today, Ryan Speedo Green is a world-famous opera star. He credits his success to two people, a teacher and a caseworker, who showed love and acceptance to an angry boy and saw potential instead of a problem.

When Jacob and Esau's father, Isaac, "was old and his eyes were so weak that he could no longer see," he called for Esau, his older son, to come to him. However, when Jacob showed up instead, Isaac did not realize it and gave him the birthright blessing. He proceeded to ask his son to "prepare . . . the kind of tasty food I like and bring it to me to eat, so that I may give you my blessing before I die" (Genesis 27:1–4).

What is this blessing? In the patriarchal period, the blessing of a dying father was transmitted to his heir. In this blessing was the power for health, prosperity, victory in battle, and wisdom. Such blessings, once invoked, could not be revoked. It was like being named in a will that could not be contested.

The significance of this blessing is evidenced by Esau's reaction when he realized he did not receive it from Isaac. He said, " 'Do you have only one blessing, my father? Bless me too, my father!' Then Esau wept aloud" (Genesis 27:38).

Overcoming dysfunction

We live in families, and we look for family blessing and approval. We can overcome dysfunctional families, as Ryan Green did, through the support and approval of other significant people in our lives. It isn't just the fact that college students call home for money that suggests they are a part of a family. Emotionally, we all live our lives either coming to terms with our family or reacting against our family.

Ellen White wrote a letter to a father who selfishly expressed no approval of his family. "Brother B is not of a temperament to bring sunshine into his family. Here is a good place for him to begin to work. He is more like a cloud than a beam of light. He is too selfish to speak words of approval to the members of his family, especially to the one of all others who should have his love and tender respect. He is morose, overbearing, dictatorial; his words are frequently cutting, and leave a wound that he does not try to heal by softening spirit, acknowledging his faults, and confessing his wrongdoings."[7]

Review your home and family, not only those under your roof but your extended family, no matter where they live. What are the ways that you might help bring health to your family? Perhaps you could speak a word of encouragement, express support, or show love? No one is an island. We are all very connected to our families and an emotional product of those family relationships.

"The LORD is slow to anger and filled with unfailing love, forgiving every kind of sin and rebellion. But he does not excuse the guilty. He lays the sins of the parents upon their children; the entire family is affected—even children in the third and fourth generations" (Numbers 14:18, NLT). The laying of the sins of the parents upon their children is not the vindictive punishment of an angry God but a simple statement of how things work.

If the problem is really the mother, then a child's decision to get married to get out of the house would solve the problem. But we know that that doesn't work. If the problem is the father, then moving away and getting a job on your own would solve the problem. But we know that that doesn't work. If the problem is really the child, then when the child moves out, the home returns to sweetness and light. But we know that that doesn't really solve the problem.

Seeking to solve problems by physical separation from the problem does not work because it does not address the heart of the issue. No parents are perfect. No children are perfect. There is only One who is perfect, and when we find our identity in Him when we receive His grace and acceptance, it frees us to be what we were created to be, vessels of grace to all those around us. Finding our identity in God frees us to develop toward His ideal rather than following a path laid out by others who may not have our best interests at heart but are seeking to use us to fix their own identity crises. Finding our identity in God enables us not to be dependent on any dysfunction of our human families for our sense of identity.

The old song "Dry Bones" is based on Ezekiel 37, where Ezekiel goes out and looks on the valley of bones.

> Ezekiel connected dem dry bones . . .
> Now hear the word of the Lord.
> Well, your toe bone connected to your foot bone
> Your foot bone connected to your heel bone
> Your heel bone connected to the ankle bone.[8]

The word in the song that emphasizes the message of the story of Jacob and Esau is "connected." Jacob and Esau were connected even when they were separated. We are all connected to our families, whether we have functional families or dysfunctional ones, and we received much of our education through our family. Jesus "came to restore, elevate, purify, and ennoble every current of pure affection, that the family on earth might become a symbol of the family in heaven."[9] Living a full life is dealing with our family connections and learning about the fact that perfect love, acceptance, and approval comes only from the unfathomable grace of God.

George Bernard Shaw is quoted as saying, "Life is no brief candle to me. It is a sort of splendid torch which I have got a hold of for the moment, and I want to make it burn as brightly as possible before handing it on to future generations."[10]

We do not have to be on our deathbed, like Isaac, to pass the torch or blessing. Maybe it is time for us to discover ways of approving and supporting each other in the family so everyone in the family can learn of a God of love. "Dear children, let's not merely say that we love each other; let us show the truth by our actions" (1 John 3:18, NLT).

In our homes, we pass the torch through the approval and acceptance of our children. We pass the covenant promise of grace—the same grace we have received. We pass the covenant by accepting and approving—by blessing—our children.

In one of Aesop's fables, an old crab speaking to her son asked, "Why do you walk sideways like that, my son? You ought to walk straight!" The young crab replied, "Show me how, dear mother, and I'll follow your example."

Fenton Forest

Once upon a time in Fenton Forest, one of Scamper the Squirrel's children, Scamp was his name, was a curious squirrel and was always looking for places to explore. His curiosity often got him into trouble. Once, he climbed all over the nest of Jackie Jay, upsetting his eggs. Another time, he almost lost his life when his exploring took him right into Freddy Fox's den. But Scamp was a fearless little squirrel and was undeterred by these experiences and continued exploring new territory and frequently getting into trouble.

One day Scamp disappeared. Well, he didn't just disappear, but on one of his excursions, he did not come back home. His family was worried and started searching for him. They had no success. They asked around the forest, but the others in the forest were of little help.

In fact, Freddy the Fox said, "Well, it serves him right for being such a troublemaker." And Jackie Jay even said that he thought the forest was better off without him.

Scamp's family reported him as missing to the Missing Fenton Forest Folk Bureau, but no one seemed very concerned. When Ears Rabbit heard that Scamp was lost, he said, "Well, I just knew he would get into serious trouble someday." Gruff the Bear said, "I've watched him grow up here in this forest, and I knew he never was much good." Some were not courageous enough to say it to the family members' faces, but they thought, *You can't expect the forest family to do your work for you, keeping track of your kids.*

But Scamper's family loved Scamp and was committed to finding Scamp no matter what. They organized a search party and systematically covered the forest from one end to the other. They finally discovered Scamp, lost, hungry, and cold. They brought him home, fed him, and warmed him up. There was rejoicing in his family. Scamp was glad to be back and said that he had learned his lesson about wandering off.

And Wise Old Owl said, "Family means no one is forgotten."

---

1. "George Bernard Shaw Quotes," BrainyQuote, https://www.brainyquote.com/quotes/george_bernard_shaw_118101.

2. "Brain Development," First Things First, accessed January 22, 2020, https://www.firstthingsfirst.org/early-childhood-matters/brain-development/.

3. National Research Council, *How People Learn: Brain, Mind, Experience, and School*, exp. ed. (Washington, DC: The National Academies Press, 2000).

4. Brian D. Ray, "Research Facts on Homeschooling," NHERI, November 27, 2019, https://www.nheri.org/research-facts-on-homeschooling/.

5. Ellen G. White, *Education* (Mountain View, CA: Pacific Press®, 1903), 33.

6. "Elon Musk, Screen Time, Ryan Speedo Green," *60 Minutes* S51, E11, 44:11, December 9, 2018, https://www.cbs.com/shows/60_minutes/video/ssIdFncaAvDxX uvWKfMbTXvSl1zbceDm/elon-musk-screen-time-ryan-speedo-green/.

7. Ellen G. White, *The Adventist Home* (Nashville, TN: Southern Publishing, 1952), 226, 227.

8. James Weldon Johnson, "Dry Bones," as recorded by the Delta Rhythm Boys (1946).

9. Ellen G. White, MS 22, 1898.

10. "George Bernard Shaw," GoodReads, https://www.goodreads.com/quotes/41166 -life-is-no-brief-candle-to-me-it-is-a.

Three

The Law as Teacher

The conversation was animated as Luke, George, and Bill talked in the hallway. A sort of excitement was in the air, and all three of them felt it. What was this strange sense of daring that caused their hearts to beat a bit faster?

"Well, don't you think that the boss has a few too many rules?" Luke suggested. "I mean, we are mature enough to know what to do without being told every step to take."

Bill wasn't sure. "I don't know what you mean by 'rules.' What rules are you talking about?"

"Come on. You can't be so naive. Do you really think that you can do what you please around here?" Luke was skeptical.

"I feel I can do what I want." Bill shrugged. "Nobody forces me to do anything."

"Really?" Luke exclaimed. "Well, you know the meeting that is called for this afternoon?"

"Yeah," said Bill.

"Well, why don't you just skip it?"

"I . . . I guess I don't want to skip it. That's all . . . I want to go."

"See?" Luke cried in triumph. "The boss has you so

hoodwinked that you think you want to do exactly what he wants you to do. You are enslaved, and you don't even know it."

"I'm not!"

"You are."

"I'm not!"

"Well, then don't go."

"OK, I won't!"

Luke's strange smile made Bill uneasy. "We will see how free you are this afternoon." And with that, Luke walked away, leaving Bill and George standing there.

George spoke first, "I'm not sure I like what I am hearing. I have never heard you talk like that before. I feel strange. I don't think we should even be talking like this."

Bill was silent for a long time before he said, "I don't know. Luke has a point. If we never do anything that the boss disapproves of, are we really free to do what we want? We may be just slaves around here—nose to the grindstone, smile when you should, do this, do that. Did you ever feel like a robot?"

"No!" George replied.

"Well, look at you," Bill said. "When was the last time you decided to do something different from what the boss wanted?"

George was silent this time. "I . . . well . . . never, I guess. I guess I never have."

"See!" Now Bill was triumphant. "You are not thinking for yourself, and you don't even know that you aren't thinking for yourself."

"But I agree with the boss."

"How do you know that you agree if you are not allowed to disagree?"

"Well, . . . I could disagree." George spoke hesitantly.

"Will you?"

"Well, . . ."

"See? You are afraid to disagree. The boss has you wrapped around his little finger."

George felt like he was being trapped. His words were being twisted, and he was getting more and more uncomfortable. "I don't like what you are saying," he said.

"And do you know why you don't like what I am saying?" Bill responded.

"No. It just seems strange."

"See, George, you are just an emotional captive to the organization. You can't think for yourself. You aren't free. You're a robot. The fact that I can ask questions and offer some criticism shows I am an independent thinker. Don't you see, George? Luke has a good point. He wants to help the boss and everyone. I think things would be much better around here if there were a little more freedom. I am going to skip that meeting this afternoon."

The meeting took place as planned, and Bill didn't go. George was present, but his mind was elsewhere. He wondered what the boss was thinking and what Bill was doing. He hadn't expected to see Luke, but there he was, all smiles. As a leader, it would have been obvious if he had missed.

The exciting thrill that Bill had experienced that morning faded a bit as he wondered what to do with himself while everyone was at the meeting. He felt uncomfortable being alone while everyone else went. He thought of getting under his desk, but what if someone saw him? That would look dumb. So he just sat and thought and wondered what was going on at the meeting.

And so it was that Luke, or Lucifer, spread discontent in the perfect heavenly environment, and the tingling excitement of sin was captivating for some. It became crystal clear to all the angels that there was a law in heaven. Lucifer claimed that there was no need for a law, that angels should be free to follow their own will rather than be bound by unnecessary restrictions. For the first time, there was conflict in heaven, and the perfect harmony of the celestial realm was broken.

"Sin originated in self-seeking. Lucifer, the covering cherub, desired to be first," Ellen White says. "He sought to gain control of heavenly beings, to draw them away from their Creator, and to win their homage to himself. Therefore, he misrepresented God, attributing to Him the desire for self-exultation."[1] Selfishness is at the core of all sin, the black hole of seeking predominance, whether in a marriage relationship, a business deal, or experiencing road rage while driving your car.

Lucifer misrepresents God

Today, Lucifer continues to portray the government of God as oppressive, the law of God as a burdensome yoke of bondage, and the will of God as dictatorial.

The law of God is not an abstract decree of a distant deity or a list of thou-shalt-nots chiseled in stone. It is an expression of who God is, an expression of his character.[2] To experience God is to experience God's law; therefore, the law is our teacher about God. To know God is to know the law and to know the law is to know God. The angels in heaven knew no law. They only knew God. They lived in harmony with the law of God because they lived in harmony with God. Ellen White says, "The principles of God's law must be kept before the people as everlasting and inexorable as the character of God himself."[3] To educate about God is to teach about God's law, and the summation of the law is love. The law describes what love looks like. The first four commandments teach us how to love God, and the last six teach us how to love our neighbor. Education, then, is teaching students about the law, which is teaching them about God. Ellen White notes that "fathers and mothers were to instruct their children that the law of God is an expression of His character, and that as they received the principles of the law into the heart, the image of God was traced on mind and soul."[4]

At an evangelistic series I attended as a child, the speaker had a memorable way of illustrating the role that the law plays in our lives. He wiped his brow with a handkerchief, placed the handkerchief back in his pocket, and continued his talk. The audience began to stir because now he had a black mark on his face that could be seen by everyone. He acted like he did not know why they were suddenly murmuring, and he asked them what the problem was. Then he took out a mirror and looked at his face, and of course, he could see the black stain. Before the meeting, he had placed some charcoal in his handkerchief to make a point. Then he would ask the audience whether it was possible to remove the stain with the mirror. When they all agreed it was not, he used some water and a clean cloth to remove the stain. The mirror only showed him the stain; something else was needed to remove it.

The mirror is the law. It can reveal what the problems are, but it doesn't remove them. The only way to remove the stain is to go to Jesus. "For what the law was powerless to do in that it was weakened by the sinful nature, God did by sending his own Son in the likeness of sinful man to be a sin offering" (Romans 8:3).

I have an owner's manual for my car. I refer to it often to make sure that I care for the car appropriately. I am free to ignore the advice and put water in the engine instead of oil, but the engine will soon be ruined. I follow the directions provided by the people who made the car. They know what will keep it running.

God is our Creator. He made us and knows what is best for us. "This is love for God: to obey his commands. And his commands are not burdensome" (1 John 5:3). Not only are His commands not burdensome, but they are also life-giving, sustaining His created beings most fully and happily.

I must admit that when I am driving a fast car, I do not always like the law. I do not want to be taught by the traffic law what is best for me. I prefer to do my own thing and drive as fast as I like. But the law teaches me that the road is narrow and has a lot of curves, and it protects me from driving at a dangerous speed.

Teaching the law without knowing the Lawgiver is dangerous. Even knowledge about the Bible without the love of God results in pride and legalism. The most significant danger of legalism is that no one sees themselves as a legalist; they may believe they are zealous Christians. The Pharisees claimed to be elevating the law, but they were debasing it because they took the commandments without knowing the Commander. The law can be dangerous in the hands of someone who does not know the Lawgiver, as dangerous as a scalpel would be in the hands of someone who has never studied surgery.

The Pharisees were not convicted of sin, for they separated the law from the author of the law. When Jesus, the author of the law, came to them, they crucified Him. Legalism is a Satan-designed trap to make people think that they are honoring the law when they are destroying it.

The Shema is the oldest fixed daily prayer in Judaism. It has been recited morning and evening since ancient times. It is called the "Shema" because *shĕma'* is the first Hebrew word in the passage. It is found in Deuteronomy and is all about the law as a teacher. "And you must love the LORD your God with all your heart, all your soul, and all your strength. And you must commit yourselves wholeheartedly to these commands that I am giving you today" (Deuteronomy 6:5, 6, NLT).

Notice how the passage ties love and commands together. They are inseparable. Teaching God's law is teaching about God. Of course, there are those whose approach to the law and methods in teaching it leave the love of God out of the picture, and the result is an unloving legalism that foments rebellion.

The law is a revelation of the will and character of its Author. God is love, and His law is love. Its two great principles are love to God and love to humankind. Ellen White says, " 'Love is the fulfilling of the law.' The character of God is righteousness and truth, and such is the nature of his law."[5]

George found Bill after the meeting. "Well, how do you feel

about your newly found freedom?"

Bill was silent.

"Did you know that Luke went to the meeting?" George pressed.

Bill looked up angrily. George felt a stab of pain in his chest as he observed Bill's unhappy emotions. George continued, "I thought that this freedom was supposed to be a glorious experience that would result in great benefit for everyone, and yet you don't seem very happy. What did you do during the meeting?"

Bill was sullen. "None of your business. I did what I wanted to."

Just then, Luke came by, and Bill said, "I didn't go to the meeting just like I told you I wouldn't, and how come you went?"

Luke said as if surprised, "Well, I never said I wasn't going to go. I just said that I didn't think you were free enough not to go."

"You tricked me!" Bill cried.

"No, no. I'm proud of you for being so independent. You and I will do great things together. You are my kind of angel. Listen, when things get sorted out around here, I think you should have a promotion and have more responsibility. You know I am responsible for placement, and I can work something out for you."

Bill softened and said, "Well, I do feel kind of good thinking for myself. I imagine that the boss needs those who think for themselves."

"Sure, he does!" said Luke, "How do you think he got where he is?"

"Well, I never thought of that," said Bill. "Do you mean to say that you think that he is where he is because he was once like us and then began to think for himself?"

"Could be," said Luke.

Education

George had listened carefully during their conversations, and now Luke turned to him. "Well, George! Pretty heady stuff, isn't it? Think you could handle it?"

George started to open his mouth but changed his mind. He turned and ran or flew.

The law is our fence, protecting us, and teaching us about God.

'Twas a dangerous cliff, as they freely confessed,
Though to walk near its crest was so pleasant;
But over its terrible edge there had slipped
A duke and full many a peasant.
So the people said something would have to be done,
But their projects did not at all tally;
Some said, "Put a fence 'round the edge of the cliff,"
Some, "An ambulance down in the valley."

But the cry for the ambulance carried the day,
For it spread through the neighboring city;
A fence may be useful or not, it is true,
But each heart became full of pity
For those who slipped over the dangerous cliff;
And the dwellers in highway and alley
Gave pounds and gave pence, not to put up a fence,
But an ambulance down in the valley.

"For the cliff is all right, if you're careful," they said,
"And, if folks even slip and are dropping,
It isn't the slipping that hurts them so much
As the shock down below when they're stopping."
So day after day, as these mishaps occurred,
Quick forth would those rescuers sally
To pick up the victims who fell off the cliff,
With their ambulance down in the valley.

The Law as Teacher

Then an old sage remarked: "It's a marvel to me
That people give far more attention
To repairing results than to stopping the cause,
When they'd much better aim at prevention.
Let us stop at its source all this mischief," cried he,
"Come, neighbors and friends, let us rally;
If the cliff we will fence, we might almost dispense
With the ambulance down in the valley."

"Oh, he's a fanatic," the others rejoined,
"Dispense with the ambulance? Never!
He'd dispense with all charities, too, if he could;
No! No! We'll support them forever.
Aren't we picking up folks just as fast as they fall?
And shall this man dictate to us? Shall he?
Why should people of sense stop to put up a fence,
While the ambulance works in the valley?"

But the sensible few, who are practical too,
Will not bear with such nonsense much longer;
They believe that prevention is better than cure,
And their party will soon be the stronger.
Encourage them then, with your purse, voice, and pen,
And while other philanthropists dally,
They will scorn all pretense, and put up a stout fence
On the cliff that hangs over the valley.

Better guide well the young than reclaim them when old,
For the voice of true wisdom is calling.
"To rescue the fallen is good, but 'tis best
To prevent other people from falling."
Better close up the source of temptation and crime
Than deliver from dungeon or galley;
Better put a strong fence 'round the top of the cliff

Than an ambulance down in the valley.[6]

1. Ellen G. White, *The Desire of Ages* (Mountain View, CA: Pacific Press®, 1940), 21, 22.

2. Ellen G. White, "The Glory of God Revealed in Mystery," *Signs of the Times*, April 23, 1896.

3. Ellen G. White, "A Lesson for the Times, Number Two," *Health Reformer*, August 1, 1878, 237.

4. White, *Desire of Ages*, 69.

5. Ellen G. White, "A Revelation of God's Will and Character," *Reflecting Christ* (Hagerstown, MD: Review and Herald®, 1985), 62.

6. Joseph Malins, "Ambulance Down in the Valley" (1895), https://www.tony cooke.org/stories-and-illustrations/ambulance_valley/.

Four

"The Eyes of the LORD"

The Biblical Worldview

"A well-known scientist (some say it was Bertrand Russell) once gave a public lecture on astronomy. He described how the earth orbits around the sun and how the sun, in turn, orbits around the center of a vast collection of stars called our galaxy. At the end of the lecture, a little old lady at the back of the room got up and said: 'What you have told us is rubbish. The world is really a flat plate supported on the back of a giant tortoise.' The scientist gave a superior smile before replying, 'What is the tortoise standing on?' 'You're very clever, young man, very clever,' said the old lady. 'But it's turtles all the way down!' "[1]

That story is from the book *A Brief History of Time* by Steven Hawking, the famous theoretical physicist. It was a popularized description of some of the implications of quantum mechanics. In his introduction to the book, Carl Sagan said, "This is also a book about God . . . or perhaps about the absence of God. The word God fills these pages. . . . Hawking is attempting, as he explicitly states, to understand the mind of God."[2]

Identity

It is not just philosophers and theologians who are exploring the existence of God; scientists are as well. As they expand our knowledge of the universe, they bump up against the question of how life began. How life began is central to our sense of identity because our beginning has implications for our ending. Is the end eternal nonexistence, or, as the Bible says, is it God dwelling with men? "And I heard a loud voice from the throne saying, 'Now the dwelling of God is with men, and he will live with them. They will be his people, and God himself will be with them and be their God' " (Revelation 21:3).

When I was a student in France participating in the Adventist Colleges Abroad program, I traveled alone to Lausanne, Switzerland. While in a hotel along the shore of Lake Geneva, the thought came to me, *Here I am, five thousand miles from home, alone in a city where nobody knows me, and I could break all the rules of the school and family, and nobody would know.* So what did I do? I went to bed and did nothing that would besmirch my family name. My identity, my family origin, led me not to want to disappoint my family or my God.

Where I came from formed my moral identity. Vital to a person's sense of identity is not only parentage but answers to the larger question of origins. Do we believe in a supreme being to whom we owe allegiance and find our identity, or are we the product of the random collision of atoms and molecules millions of years ago? Many voices are seeking to answer these questions today. In the end, there are only two answers. As Henry Morris says, "All things either can—or cannot—be explained in terms of a self-contained universe by ongoing natural processes. If they can, then evolution is true. If they cannot, then they must be explained, at least in part, by completed extra-natural processes in a universe which itself was created."[3]

A biblical worldview

A person's worldview, or philosophy of life, has a significant impact on a person's identity and moral perspective. The naturalistic evolutionary approach to existence provided by public higher education reflects the post-Christian culture. Seventh-day Adventist education offers students a biblical worldview that answers life's fundamental questions of origins with a personal Creator God at the center. Is it possible in this scientific age to maintain a biblical worldview? Peter predicted that there would be a time when the world would ridicule those who maintained a biblical worldview. "First of all, you must understand that in the last days scoffers will come, scoffing and following their own evil desires. They will say, 'Where is this "coming" he promised? Ever since our fathers died, everything goes on as it has since the beginning of creation' " (2 Peter 3:3, 4).

Today we have clear manifestations of that ridicule in public education that prohibits the teaching of Creation. Unfortunately, the church over the ages has frequently fallen into the trap of affirming more than the Bible required, making the person with the biblical worldview look unintelligent. Early in the history of civilization, anything not understood was attributed to the miraculous intervention of God or gods. Everything that could not easily be explained was a miracle. People were called infidels and atheists when they explained things by natural laws. Scientists, through observation and experiment, began discerning how things worked and developed laws of science.

The church called chemistry one of the "seven devilish arts" because it presumed to explain the cause of things, so God was not the cause. In the thirteenth century, when Roger Bacon claimed that the rainbow resulted from the refraction of light, he was condemned "on account of certain suspicious novelties." Of course, the rainbow was a sign from God and, therefore, could not result from natural laws. There was opposition to placing lightning rods on churches because it was "attempting to control the artillery of heaven."

In the early 1960s, some claimed "on biblical authority" that humans would never land on the moon. They fell into the trap of asking more of the Bible than is required. It is not necessary to say that Adam was created at 9:00 A.M. on October 23, 4004 BC, as does Archbishop Usher. The Bible does not demand that. You cannot date Creation by adding up biblical genealogies. Nor does the Bible demand fixity of species. One of the reasons Darwin developed the idea of evolution was that the church at the time took Scripture to mean that species were fixed. They based it on the Genesis phrase "after its kind." Darwin went out into the field and simply found that it was not true. We must be careful not to make the Bible say more than it says.

Having a biblical worldview is not incompatible with the scientific method. The Bible is not a piece of scientific literature, but that does not mean it is incompatible with true science. It does mean that we should not require too much of a book that was written in a different era in a different language for a different purpose. The message we get from the Bible is not primarily scientific but salvific. Its focus is the salvation story.

The loss of a biblical worldview has uprooted the moral foundation of society. On what basis can one make moral decisions when there is no basis for morality, or when there is no standard to appeal to, or when a person's identity is whatever a person wants it to be without any external frame of reference? Our world is much like Israel during the time of the judges, when the nation had no king. "In those days Israel had no king; everyone did as he saw fit" (Judges 17:6).

An exclusively scientific worldview results in culture and society with no moral standard or foundation. The law of God is null and void. The following statement by Jeremy Rifkin describes the result of an exclusively scientific worldview:

We no longer feel ourselves to be guests in someone else's home and therefore obliged to make our behavior conform with a set of pre-existing cosmic rules. It is our creation now. We make the rules. We establish the parameters of reality. We create the world, and because we do, we no longer feel beholden to outside forces. We no longer have to justify our behavior, for we are now the architects of the universe. We are responsible to nothing outside ourselves, for we are the kingdom, the power, and the glory forever and ever.[4]

Can we be intellectually honest as we live in a world of scientific scoffers? How can we live as people of faith in a scientific world? Choosing either worldview—one based on the Bible or one based on evolution—requires faith. "It is not possible to prove, in the experimental sense, either evolution or creation, since we can neither observe past history directly nor reproduce it in the laboratory."[5]

In his closing chapter of *A Brief History of Time*, Steven Hawking repeats the basic questions: "We find ourselves in a bewildering world. We want to make sense of what we see around us and to ask:

- What is the nature of the universe?
- What is our place in it, and where did it and we come from?
- Why is it the way it is?"[6]

Hawking and many scientists who seek to understand the universe without considering God come up against an impossibility of something coming from nothing. It takes a great deal of faith to believe that the universe and all human life came from nothing.

Education

Everyone has faith in something

A story is told of a man who wanted to study deep-sea life, and he used a net that had a mesh of three inches. He caught many things and then concluded that there were no deep-sea fish smaller than three inches in length. Using just the scientific net to catch truth does not allow for catching evidence of the spirit.[7]

More is going on in the universe than what can be placed in a test tube or under a microscope. It is like seeking to understand a four-dimensional world when you live in a three-dimensional world. There are things that we cannot explain through the scientific method, such as love, beauty, human consciousness, and morality. Faith is a way of knowing something that cannot be known through test-tube experimentation.

We all confront life's questions. What is the aim of my life? What is its origin? What is its meaning? Everyone has faith, either in the turtle theory, the natural evolution theory, the Creator God theory, or whatever. One way or another, we are going by faith. So I choose to accept by faith a biblical worldview. "By the word of the LORD were the heavens made, their starry host by the breath of his mouth" (Psalm 33:6). That belief makes all the difference.

You have heard the expression, "Well, you would understand if you knew where they came from." It is a way of explaining the behavior of some people. It is suggesting that if you understood their background, then you would not be too quick to pass judgment on their behavior. Nothing is more important to a person's sense of identity as their sense of origin, their family. Having a biblical worldview provides me with an identity that tells me who I am.

I have twins and occasionally get them confused. I once asked my daughter, "Who are you?"

"Julie," she said.

"But who is that?" I pestered.

"Me," she said with some confusion.

Again, I asked, "Who are you?"

"Julie," she responded again. And as I continued to press her, she finally said in exasperation, "I am your daughter!" That is who she is, my daughter. It is there that she finds identity.

The doctrine of Creation gives us our ultimate identity as children of God. In our belief in a Creator God, we find our deepest heritage and moral frame of reference. If the "survival of the fittest"[8] comprises our frame of reference, then anything that gives us prominence and power over others is acceptable. But that is Lucifer's approach of self-exaltation, which contrasts radically with Jesus' approach, "who, being in very nature God, did not consider equality with God something to be grasped, but made himself nothing, taking the very nature of a servant, being made in human likeness. And being found in appearance as a man, he humbled himself and became obedient to death— even death on a cross!" (Philippians 2:5–8).

Those who would choose the path of theistic evolution to combine belief in God and evolution have a difficult time with God's taking millions of years to create humankind and yet resurrect Lazarus in one day. Why would God take millions of years to bring from the primordial ooze of the swamp the first life-forms that would become human and yet resurrect from the dust of the earth people at the Second Coming? "In a moment, in the twinkling of an eye, at the last trump: for the trumpet shall sound, and the dead shall be raised incorruptible, and we shall be changed" (1 Corinthians 15:52, KJV).

I would agree with Thomas Aquinas, who said, "Believing in God, and not believing that he is the Creator, would mean not believing that God exists, at all."[9]

Fenton Forest

Once upon a time in Fenton Forest, there was a great tragedy. A severe storm swept over Fenton Forest, and one of the large trees that held the nest of a bluebird family was blown down.

Education

At the end of the storm, the Fenton Forest folk emerged from their various homes to evaluate the damage that occurred to the forest. Soon they realized that one whole family of bluebirds was killed.

Everyone gathered at the base of the tree where the tragedy occurred. As they were sifting through the remains of the home, they found one egg that had not been crushed in the fall. It was under the dead body of the mother bluebird and was still warm.

What would they do? While they were trying to decide what to do about this egg, the egg was getting cold. Well, Gruff's little cub, Blacky, wasn't going to wait for a committee decision on what to do with the egg! He took the egg carefully in his paws, and while the others were busy talking, he carefully carried it to his den and found a place where he could keep it. He kept the little bluebird egg warm and carefully watched over it until finally, one day, it hatched.

Blacky was so happy. He did a wonderful job feeding the hatchling. He enlisted the help of Randy Raccoon in getting some worms, and he asked Jackie Jay exactly how he should feed the little bluebird. In a few short months, this little bluebird was hopping all around Gruff's bear den.

Gruff and his family did their best to care for the little bluebird, but the poor thing was trying to act like a bear. She managed to imitate a growl and tried to be like the only parents she knew. It was a hopeless task. She wasn't born to be a bear, and it was very frustrating. She knew something was wrong, and she thought the problem was with her. She couldn't do anything that the other bear cubs did, no matter how she tried.

She became more and more discouraged with life in Gruff's den until one day, one glorious day, a bluebird came to Fenton Forest and visited the little bird in Gruff's den. It was then that the baby bluebird saw what she was created to be, and she stopped trying to be a bear. Wise Old Owl said, "When you know where you come from, you know who you are."

1. Steven Hawking, *A Brief History of Time* (New York: Bantam Books, 1988), 1.

2. Hawking, *A Brief History of Time*, x.

3. Henry M. Morris, *What Is Creation Science* (Green Forest, AR: Master Books, 1987), 14, https://www.masterbooks.com/mwdownloads/download/link/id/956/.

4. Morris, *What Is Creation Science*, 49, 50.

5. Morris, *What Is Creation Science*, 30.

6. Hawking, *A Brief History of Time*, 171.

7. Morris, *What Is Creation Science*.

8. "Survival of the fittest" is a phrase that originated from Darwinian evolutionary theory as a way of describing the mechanism of natural selection.

9. Christoph Cardinal Schönborn, *Chance or Purpose? Creation, Evolution, and a Rational Faith*, ed. Hubert Philip Weber, trans. Henry Taylor (San Francisco: Ignatius Press, 2007), 17.

Five

Jesus as the Master Teacher

Once upon a time, there was a school. It was a fine school, and it had a wonderful faculty. One member of the faculty was the teacher in the sixth-grade room. This teacher was the epitome of good teachers, from all appearances. The Immaculate, Organized Teacher. This teacher's room was always the showplace of the school. It seemed as if the idea of bulletin boards originated there; for each week, there was a new creative one decorating the wall. The carpeted floors were always immaculate, and a pencil mark on a desk or wall could not have survived more than five minutes. The other teachers in the school were quietly envious of the perfect control that this teacher seemed to have over everything connected with the sixth-grade room. Daily lesson plans, weekly lesson plans, and yearly lesson plans with behavioral objectives outlined in detail were always on the principal's desk before the beginning of the school year. While other teachers were rushing around at the last minute putting together their rooms, this teacher would relax, visit with parents, and study because her room was always ready a week or two before school started.

There was a boy named Freddy who was in the sixth grade.

He was a little different and did not fit into the finely tuned program of the sixth-grade room. He did not come from a neat home and never measured up to the level of cleanliness that was the standard of the Immaculate, Organized Teacher. He was a little overweight and was teased by the other kids in the school. The teacher was frequently exasperated with him. He would eat crumbly cookies and gooey chocolate at his desk, and there was hardly a lunch that passed that did not result in some mess to clean up where Freddy had eaten. He did not dress too well, and of course, his success in school was hardly measurable. Homework would be returned with enough peanut butter on it to make an adequate sandwich. Freddy's low position in the eyes of the class was reflected in the position that the boys gave him in their own pecking order. On the occasions when Freddy was sick and stayed home, it seemed that everything went much smoother in the classroom. The Immaculate, Organized Teacher was tired of Freddy and secretly wished that he would withdraw from school. It would make things so much easier for everyone.

And it came to pass that Saint Peter called Freddy, and he was carried by the angels straight to heaven, where he was placed in the heavenly schoolroom right next to the Model Teacher himself. Saint Peter also called the Immaculate, Organized Teacher, but she ended up in hell. Being in torment, the Immaculate, Organized Teacher looked up and saw Freddy way up in the heavenly schoolroom with the Model Teacher. He was busily working on his assignments, and the teacher cried out and said, "Model Teacher, have mercy on me. Send Freddy that he may dip the tip of his finger in the water and cool my tongue; for I am tormented in this flame." But the Model Teacher said, "Immaculate, Organized Teacher—remember that when you were alive, you had all that you wanted—a modern classroom, excellent lesson plans, and lots of equipment. And remember how you did not think Freddy fit into your smooth, finely tuned program. How he never had his lessons done and could never do them right or get much help. So now he is here, getting help on his lessons and getting the recognition that he never was able to get from you, and you are in anguish. And besides all that, there is a chasm between us, and no one can cross it going either direction."

Then Immaculate, Organized Teacher said, "Please send him to my conference, to the education department, for I have many fellow teachers whom he can warn about this place of torment lest they come here when they die."

Then the Model Teacher said, "They already have the education code, Ellen White, and the Bible. They can get the message from them."

And the Immaculate, Organized Teacher said, "No—if one went to them from the dead, they would repent."

And the Model Teacher said, "If they do not read and listen to the Bible and the Spirit of Prophecy, neither will they be persuaded even though someone rises from the dead" (see Luke 16).

Is there anything wrong with an immaculate, organized teacher who has lesson plans and behavioral objectives? No, certainly not! And this Freddy has real problems. He will never be a brilliant star. There is nothing about Freddy to commend him to the teacher except his need—his desperate, crying need.

The Immaculate, Organized Teacher would be featured in the education magazine. The accreditation committee would have only good to say about this teacher and the sixth-grade room. There is nothing bad about the teacher except for not responding to a desperate, crying need.

And Jesus said to them, "It is not the healthy who need a doctor, but the sick. I have not come to call the righteous, but sinners" (Mark 2:17). As Ellen White says, everything Jesus did in His life on earth had a single purpose: "the revelation of God for the uplifting of humanity."[1]

Education

Jesus was a teacher and a student

Jesus is the Master Teacher, but He was first a master student. We must first be students ourselves—as Christ was a student. "And Jesus increased in wisdom and stature, and in favour with God and man" (Luke 2:52, KJV). Jesus was a student in three important ways, and we also need to be students in those ways.

First, Jesus increased in wisdom; He was a student of Himself. Second, Jesus increased in favor with God; He was a student of God. Third, Jesus increased in favor with humans; He was a student of people.

How was Jesus a student of Himself? He spent the first and largest portion of His life answering the questions "Who am I? What am I here for?"

> His [Jesus'] education was gained from Heaven-appointed sources, from useful work, from the study of the Scriptures, from nature, and from the experiences of life—God's lesson books, full of instruction to all who bring to them the willing hand, the seeing eye, and the understanding heart. . . .
>
> Thus to Jesus the significance of the Word and the works of God was unfolded, as He was trying to understand the reason of things.[2]

All humanity is seeking to answer the question of personal identity. Until we are students enough to answer the question "Who am I?" we will not be able to help others. As Socrates said, "Know thyself." Arthur Holmes put the question in the context of education. "The question to ask about education, then, is not 'What can I do with all this stuff anyway?' because both I and my world are changing, but rather 'What will all this stuff do to me?' This question is basic to the concept of liberal education."[3]

A Christian education does more than provide facts and skills to get a job. Through mentors and other Christian peers, it develops Christian maturity, bringing changes to the heart. We need to know ourselves; being a student of self enables us to put life's difficulties in perspective. Jesus knew Himself and was not threatened by pharisaical criticism or the praise of the crowds. Do I know myself and my emotions so that I am more concerned about the Freddys in my life than about my reputation? Do I know myself enough so that the Freddys in my life are more important than my perfectionism? "To know one's self is great knowledge. True self-knowledge will lead to a humility that will allow the Lord to train the mind, and mold and discipline the character."[4]

Second, how was Jesus a student of God? We do not think much about Christ being a student of God, but He did not have all His knowledge just poured into Him at birth or baptism. He learned in the same way we learn. "His intimate acquaintance with the Scriptures shows how diligently His early years were given to the study of God's Word. And spread out before Him was the great library of God's created works. He who had made all things studied the lessons which His own hand had written in earth and sea and sky."[5]

We know and understand ourselves by being a students of God. We cannot know ourselves until we know our Creator. He learned of His identity from the same material that we have available to us, the Bible. And so, we truly know ourselves as we know and become students of God. Are we spending our lives seeking to find out more about Him so that we can understand who we are? Christian education is only Christian to the extent that we are students of God, for to know God is eternal life.

Finally, how was Jesus a student of people? Abraham Lincoln is supposed to have said, "I do not like that man. I must get to know him better."[6] Each of my twin daughters, though they live on opposite sides of the country, made a close friendship with a very needy person. Both of the people they met were

Education

alcoholics, and one of them was a homeless person living in an orange grove. They arranged to do things for them, such as providing a birthday cake, giving a haircut, and doing laundry. It would be easy to judge these gentlemen based on their dress, drunken behavior, and lack of being gainfully employed—easy until you heard their stories. The homeless man had an abusive father who once killed his son's cat and made him eat it. The other man saw his two brothers killed when he was young, was physically abused, and had PTSD (post-traumatic stress disorder) from what he saw and did in his military service. The pilgrim John Bradford allegedly spoke the words, " 'There but for the grace of God, goes John Bradford,' in reference to a group of prisoners being led to execution."[7] We need to be reminded to think before we criticize or judge someone. Everyone who we meet has traveled a path different from ours, and until we seek to understand their path, we will be quick to judge them because they do not meet our standard. A Native American is purported to have said, "Do not judge someone until you have walked a mile in their moccasins."

Imagine that you have accidentally hit a dog with your car—not so hard as to kill the dog but enough to injure it. You responsibly get out of your car and go over to the dog to help it. What is the dog's response when you reach out to help it? Most likely, it will bite you. When we come across people who are angry and hostile, our first thought must not be *That is a bad person!* but rather, *I wonder what pain this person is experiencing in life?*

Jesus was a student before He became a teacher. He was a student of life, of people. He knew people. He knew where they were coming from. You do not find Jesus being distracted by smoke screens. As we see Him talking to the woman at Jacob's well, she throws up smoke screen after smoke screen. (See John 4.)

"You are a Jew, and I am a Samaritan woman. How can you ask me for a drink?" (verse 9).

"Are you greater than our father Jacob?" (verse 12).

54

"Our fathers worshiped on this mountain, but you Jews claim that the place where we must worship is in Jerusalem" (verse 20).

Jesus refused to fight; He knew Himself, He knew God, and He knew people. He knew her need and would not be distracted. This knowledge of people was not simply a divine gift, something only He could have. We all would judge others less if we listened to people's stories more.

Jesus, the Model Teacher, understood where His students lived. It does not take brilliance to be a student of people. When people talk, listen completely. The way to show respect to another person is to listen to what they have to say. It does not take a master's degree in counseling or psychology; it does take love. It does mean living outside our selfishness, which is possible when we have been a student of self and of God.

Fenton Forest

Once upon a time in Fenton Forest, Freddy the Fox came home from a long journey. He had been traveling through many unknown forests and shared with everyone what a wonderful trip he had enjoyed. Freddy loved to travel, and on this trip, he traveled farther then he had ever traveled before.

A few weeks after Freddy returned, he felt sick. His sickness started with a headache and then progressed to his limbs. He was so sick it was difficult for him to walk. Other Fenton Forest folks, not knowing where he had been or what disease he might have picked up during his travels, didn't go close to him. They were afraid that whatever his sickness was, it might be catching.

Freddy got so sick that he was unable to get food for himself. He could hardly move. Everyone in the forest began talking about poor Freddy. They discussed what his disease might be. They even had a Fenton Forest Council meeting and formed some committees to decide what to do about his problem. Gruff the Bear's committee decided that it would endanger the whole forest if his disease spread, and so they suggested that he be asked to leave Fenton Forest until he got better. Of course, he couldn't leave because he was so weak, he couldn't walk. Another committee suggested that they put up signs all around Freddy's den that read, "Danger! Quarantined Fox!" The signs were posted, and no one got close to Freddy. Anytime one of the Fenton Forest children sneezed or coughed, their parents would say, "Have you been by Freddy's den? Stay away from him; he is quarantined."

With all the forest folks avoiding Freddy like the plague, he was not getting enough to eat. He was drinking no water, and he was getting worse quickly. The weaker Freddy got, the more the Fenton Forest folk talked about him and expressed concern. Their expressions of concern were not so much for Freddy's health as they were concern that they did not catch his terrible disease.

One day Ears Rabbit, who was not exactly a good friend of Freddy, went by his den and heard Freddy moaning and groaning. He was worried about the quarantine signs, but he stopped in anyway, mostly from curiosity. When he saw Freddy, he ran home and brought Freddy some water and food. He worked around and cleaned up his den a bit. He went to Grandma Rabbit and got some medicine leaves she recommended for "most anything that ailed you." Ears Rabbit gave the medicine to Freddy and took care of him.

Other forest folks said to Ears, "Aren't you worried that you will catch his disease?"

"Yes, I guess I am," said Ears, "but when my neighbor is sick, I am sick." In a few short weeks, under the watchful care of Ears, Freddy regained his strength and, believe it or not, much to everyone's surprise, became friends with Ears Rabbit.

Wise Old Owl said, "Nobody cares how much you know until they know how much you care." (See James 2:14–17.)

1. Ellen G. White, *Education* (Mountain View, CA: Pacific Press®, 1903), 82.

2. Ellen G. White, *Child Guidance* (Nashville, TN: Southern Publishing, 1954), 50, 51.

3. Arthur F. Holmes, *The Idea of a Christian College*, rev. ed. (Grand Rapids, MI: Eerdmans, 1987), 24.

4. Ellen G. White, *Fundamentals of Christian Education* (Nashville, TN: Southern Publishing, 1923), 525.

5. White, *Child Guidance*, 50.

6. "Understanding Others," GoodReads, https://www.goodreads.com/quotes/tag /understanding-others.

7. Wiktionary, s.v. "There but for the grace of God go I," last modified June 27, 2019, 14:00, https://en.wiktionary.org/wiki/there_but_for_the_grace_of_God_go_I.

Six

More Lessons From the Master Teacher

"Stop deceiving yourselves. If you think you are wise by this world's standards, you need to become a fool to be truly wise" (1 Corinthians 3:18, NLT).

We have tests to compare ourselves with others, and when we rank in the upper 10 percent, we think we are wise, but are we? If the average ACT scores in our schools were high, would we think our schools superior? What suggestion does Paul have for the person who thinks that he or she is wise by the standards of this age? "He should become a 'fool' so that he may become wise" (verse 18). How do you become a fool? Is Paul suggesting that we forget what information we know? Is Paul talking about not being able to answer any questions on *Jeopardy*, or getting a low SAT score?

Godly wisdom

Wisdom and foolishness are being used here in a particular way. This wisdom is not understanding how computers work or being able to explain the Industrial Revolution. Paul, who was Ivy League educated, is not suggesting that you are only ready for true wisdom when you cannot answer the question

"Who was buried in Grant's tomb?" Paul is saying that wisdom is more than information. Wisdom by the standards of the age is not the true test of wisdom. It may help you pass exams and even get you a job where you make a lot of money, but it does not give life meaning. Information without a moral and ethical frame of reference leaves us with no guidance on using the information. As Paul says, "For although they knew God, they neither glorified him as God nor gave thanks to him, but their thinking became futile and their foolish hearts were darkened. Although they claimed to be wise, they became fools" (Romans 1:21, 22).

There are many fools in this post-Christian world where truth is whatever a person wants it to be. Each person chooses their own fruit from the tree of life, ignoring their Creator. When feelings are the only standard of behavior, the world descends into chaos, where people "exchanged the truth about God for a lie" (verse 25, ESV).

Worldly wisdom is what Solomon pursued. "I devoted myself to study and to explore by wisdom all that is done under heaven. . . . I have seen all the things that are done under the sun." However, he considered all of it "meaningless, a chasing after the wind" (Ecclesiastes 1:13, 14). We may be able to answer the question "Who was buried in Grant's tomb?" But what difference does it make? And if the question is considerably more significant, such as "What is the nature and origin of black holes?" then the contrast is starker still. "Do not deceive yourselves. If any one of you thinks he is wise by the standards of this age" (1 Corinthians 3:18). We are following the standards of the age when we are so degree conscious that the letters after the name mean more than the name. Obtaining an expensive Ivy League education can tempt us to find our value in what the world values.

Why did Solomon call it a chasing after the wind?

> Yet when I surveyed all that my hands had done
>> and what I had toiled to achieve,
> everything was meaningless, a chasing after the wind;
>> nothing was gained under the sun (Ecclesiastics 2:11).

Adam and Eve sought to cover their nakedness after eating from the forbidden tree. No longer seeking God's fellowship, they hid from Him. Today, some seek to promote themselves by covering their insecurities with another degree, money, or power (see 2 Corinthians 11:18). The pursuit of that which exalts a person in the eyes of secular society will never satisfy any more than the idols that the fools of Paul's time worshiped (see Acts 17:22, 23). "The fear of the LORD is the beginning of wisdom, and knowledge of the Holy One is understanding" (Proverbs 9:10).

True wisdom

Too many colleges and universities are professionalized information communication systems that seek to provide a job rather than building character. There is a lot of "chasing after the wind" in many schools. We live in an age of considerable availability of facts and information. The internet has made information available to anyone with a computer. "Nothing in education is so astonishing as the amount of ignorance it accumulates in the form of inert facts."[1]

But information doesn't provide wisdom, and it seems that the more information that is available, the less wisdom people have. True education is to give meaning to life. Jesus Christ, the Master Teacher, gives meaning to life. It is not abstract information about the universe; rather, it is relevant information about who I am and why I am here, and that wisdom comes from the Lord. "For the LORD gives wisdom, and from his mouth come knowledge and understanding" (Proverbs 2:6). What is true about the wisdom of the world is also true about the knowledge of religion. The accumulation of religious truth, no matter how true; the collection of religious facts, no matter how accurate, is no different from the worldly wisdom that is "a chasing after the wind" if not practiced in life. If we were to substitute the word *Adventist* for *Jew* in Romans 2:17–24, it might read like this: Now you, if you call yourself an Adventist; if you rely on church membership and brag about being the remnant; if you know His will and approve of what is superior because you are instructed by the law and the testimony; if you are convinced that you are a guide for the blind in healthful living, a light for those who are in the dark about the state of the dead, an instructor of the foolish who don't understand eschatology, a teacher of infants because you have in the Spirit of Prophecy an embodiment of knowledge and truth—you, then, who teach others, do you not teach yourself? You who preach against stealing, do you steal? You who say that people should not commit adultery, do you commit adultery? You who brag about the law, do you dishonor God by breaking the law? As it is written: "God's name is blasphemed among the Gentiles because of you" (compare Isaiah 52:5; Ezekiel 36:22).

Why is God's name blasphemed? Claiming truth as a possession but not living the truth is blaspheming. Blaspheming is not just swearing or taking the Lord's name in vain. It is to claim the name of Christ and not be changed by the name. Claiming to be God's remnant people because we possess truth is like Adam and Eve seeking to cover their nakedness with fig leaves. Professing the truth without living the truth is to blaspheme. Ellen White said, "Many who profess to be Christ's followers are unwilling to closely examine their own hearts, to see whether they have passed from death unto life. Some lean upon an old experience, seeming to think a mere profession of the truth will save them; but God's word reveals the terrible fact that all such are cherishing a false hope."[2] Education that is the communication of the facts of life without the wisdom of living is not true education; it is foolishness, a chasing after the wind.

Jesus makes the same point as Paul in Luke 11:52: "Woe to you experts in the law, because you have taken away the key to knowledge. You yourselves have not entered, and you have hindered those who were entering." The experts in religious knowledge, the preachers, and the teachers took away the key to knowledge. They stood around with the key and would not open the door. They had the key—they did not use it themselves, and they did not share it with others. The Master Teacher focused on what was important. "Christ could have imparted to men knowledge that would have surpassed any previous disclosures, and put in the background every other discovery, He could have unlocked mystery after mystery, and could have concentrated around these wonderful revelations the active, earnest thought of successive generations till the close of time. But He would not spare a moment from teaching the science of salvation."[3]

So what makes Christian education? Christian education is not two angels plus two angels equal four angels; it is not studying the geography of the Holy Land nor studying the Bible instead of Shakespeare. It is not different merely because of the facts dispensed. The young people learn the same math, geography, and English. It is different because Jesus, the Creator, is at the center. A Christian school doesn't just combine correct knowledge with isolating students from the world because Christians know that evil is really a matter of the heart. It is the teachers who dispense the knowledge, the peers[4] who support that knowledge, and the Christian environment in which those facts are learned that make it Christian. Jesus taught us about God when He came as God incarnate. "So the Word became human and made his home among us" (John 1:14, NLT). And so students see Jesus in the faculty and staff as they bring Jesus into focus in their own lives.

The question to ask about the college or university is not the average ACT score of those in attendance or how many Nobel prizes the faculty have received, but what kind of students does the institution attract? Are they seeking wisdom or just chasing after the wind?

Early in Christ's ministry, the disciples of John the Baptist came to see Him. They were discouraged and dejected. Their leader was in jail, and John himself had some questions. "When John heard in prison what Christ was doing, he sent his disciples to ask him, 'Are you the one who was to come, or should we expect someone else?' " (Matthew 11:2).

Jesus usually had a ready response for such questions, but not this time. Jesus just continued working, opening blind eyes, healing leprosy, delivering demoniacs, healing disease, and teaching the people. At the end of the day, He replied, "Go back and report to John what you hear and see" (Matthew 11:4).

Jesus didn't give them a Bible study proving He was the Messiah. He didn't say, "You should just trust Me." Nor did He say, "What is the matter with you; why do you doubt so soon?" No, Jesus kept working and, at the end of the day, said, "Go and tell John what you have seen."

Do we have a Christian school? It is not determined by the name or even the curriculum. It is not determined by the fact that it is sponsored by a church. The test is more objective: "Come and see!" Watch students share their faith, notice students having prayer with each other on the sidewalk, listen to the faculty share their faith and teach subjects from a biblical perspective. Watch the school family get involved in community projects.

What did John's disciples see? "The blind receive sight, the lame walk, those who have leprosy are cured, the deaf hear, the dead are raised, and the good news is preached to the poor" (Matthew 11:5).

It is not by theory that we are Christian; it is by experiencing Jesus' life in our life. Education is being with Jesus, the Master

Teacher. The disciples were not highly educated. They were fishermen, common laborers. They did not even have an eighth grade education. In Acts 4:5, there is a description of the disciples meeting with the intelligentsia of the Jewish leaders; these were those who had attended the Jewish Ivy League universities of their day. "The next day the rulers, elders and teachers of the law met in Jerusalem. Annas the high priest was there, and so were Caiaphas, John, Alexander and the other men of the high priest's family." This was a meeting of the power brokers in Jerusalem. It was a joint meeting of the senate and the house with the president in attendance.

"They had Peter and John brought before them and began to question them" (verse 7). The meeting was an inquisition. The best and brightest were quizzing these fishermen, and the record reads, "When they saw the courage of Peter and John and realized that they were unschooled, ordinary men, they were astonished, and they took note that these men had been with Jesus" (verse 13).

That is true wisdom. That is true education. That is what is of eternal significance. When you have a Christian education, other people see that you have courage, and they take note that you have been with Jesus. If education is to be of infinite value, it must put one in touch with the Infinite.

Fenton Forest

Bert, a bear of Fenton Forest, loved honey. So he decided that he would study up on honey and how it was manufactured. Now when Bert decided to do something, he never did it halfway. He spent days with a comb of honey, studying the intricate construction techniques. He studied in the field, he studied at Big Tree Tech., he studied in the library, he studied in his den.

He was getting his PhD in honeyology. He was always researching some new thing about bees and honey. You could ask him anything about honey and bees, and he knew the answer. Gruff the Bear came to him one day with honey dripping out of his mouth and over his jowls. "Come on," he invited; "I found a hive, and it is really good."

"I can't go now," replied Bert. "I just learned some new information on hive construction."

"Hive construction!" Gruff said, gruffly. "Forget it! Come with me for some hive destruction—let's eat!"

"No!" said Bert. "I need to learn this!"

So Gruff went off to eat, and Bert memorized the geometry of wax cells. And Wise Old Owl said, "Knowledge may fill the mind, but it isn't worth much unless it also fills the stomach." And so even religious knowledge may fill the mind, but until it fills the heart, it is worthless, "a chasing after the wind."

---

1. Henry Adams, *The Education of Henry Adams: An Autobiography* (Boston: Houghton Mifflin, 1918), 379.

2. Ellen G. White, "The Trial of Our Faith," *Advent Review and Sabbath Herald*, April 8, 1880, 1.

3. Ellen G. White, *The Ministry of Healing* (Mountain View, CA: Pacific Press®, 1942), 448.

4. *"The student's peer group is the single most potent source of influence on growth and development during the undergraduate years."* Alexander Astin, *What Matters in College? Four Critical Years Revisited* (San Francisco: Jossey-Bass, 1997), 398; emphasis in original.

Seven

Worship in Education

Daniel and his comrades did not have a great education by the standards of the world, so Nebuchadnezzar gave them the best that the world had to offer. " 'Select only strong, healthy, and good-looking young men,' [Nebuchadnezzar] said. 'Make sure they are well versed in every branch of learning, are gifted with knowledge and good judgment, and are suited to serve in the royal palace. Train these young men in the language and literature of Babylon' " (Daniel 1:4, NLT).

Tested in Babylon

Nebuchadnezzar had broken into their comfortable world of religious conformity in Jerusalem with his military machine and taken them to the University of Babylon. Now they were to eat pork chops instead of vegetables, drink wine instead of water, and be eunuchs instead of settling down and marrying nice Jewish girls. What had been a peaceful world for Daniel, Mishael, Hananiah, and Azariah became a vast void that threatened their identity. Even their names were changed to identify them with heathen gods. Daniel became Belteshazzar, meaning "god Bell protect the life of the king." Azariah became

Abednego—meaning "servant of the god Nabu." Their protected environment of restricted religious choices became a religiously pluralistic world with a potluck of options. The rustic little country town in Palestine was exchanged for the big city.

How were these young Hebrew boys to handle being broken out of their cocoon of Jewish cultural comfort into the Babylonian world? They started by making a deal with the attendant who had been appointed by the chief of staff to look after them. They passed this ten-day test of not eating the king's food with flying colors. He found them to be "ten times more capable" (verse 20, NLT) than the competition, enabling them to maintain their dietary lifestyle in Babylon.

Another test of their willingness to conform to the Babylonian culture came when the king erected a gold statue, ninety feet tall and nine feet wide, on the plain of Dura. He then sent out word to everyone that at the dedication ceremony, all were to bow down and worship the statue. A challenge for governments, businesses, and churches is to bring unity among the people, and Nebuchadnezzar felt he had found the perfect unifying activity. If all worshiped the same god, especially if he was the god, it would make things go much more smoothly in his kingdom.

The time came for the dedication ceremony, the moment of unity through worship in Babylon. The word went out from the king: "Whoever does not fall down and worship shall immediately be thrown into a furnace of blazing fire" (Daniel 3:6, NRSV).

The orchestra played, signaling the beginning of the worship service. Everyone fell to the ground and worshiped, save the three Hebrew worthies: Shadrach, Meshach, and Abednego. Recent graduates from Jerusalem, they ignored the king's instructions and stood straight and tall. The masses fell on their faces, leaving three solitary figures on the horizon.

This act of disobedience was reported to the king, who figured that these Hebrew boys might be hard of hearing. He generously decided to give them a second chance, warning them again about the hot furnace they would get if they disobeyed. I imagine he said something like this when he addressed them. "Listen, this statue idea came to me from your buddy, Daniel, when he interpreted my dream. You don't have to believe, just bow down and think whatever you want. Kneel and tie your sandals when the music plays. I like you guys and don't want to hurt you, but you know I will have to follow through on my command, or I will lose face."

Amazingly, Shadrach, Meshach, and Abednego did not want a second chance. They were firm in their resolve and unwavering in their decision. "O Nebuchadnezzar, we do not need to defend ourselves before you. If we are thrown into the blazing furnace, the God whom we serve is able to save us. He will rescue us from your power, Your Majesty. But even if he doesn't, we want to make it clear to you, Your Majesty, that we will never serve your gods or worship the gold statue you have set up" (verses 16–18, NLT).

They were standing on principle, saying to the king, "You may have captured our bodies, but our hearts are in Jerusalem." This was the prisoner writing on the prison walls, "Resistance." Shadrach, Meshach, and Abednego were denying the religions of the ancient world, and the authority of the king.

> Stone Walls do not a Prison make,
> Nor Iron bars a Cage;
> Minds innocent and quiet take
> That for an Hermitage;
> If I have freedom in my Love
> And in my soul am free,
> Angels alone, that soar above,
> Enjoy such Liberty.[1]

Their worship was not based on external demands but on an internal commitment to the true God. King Nebuchadnezzar warned them, "But if you do not worship it, you will be thrown immediately into a blazing furnace. Then what god will be able to rescue you from my hand?" (verse 15).

Faith in God

The gods of the ancients were there to make it easy on their followers. When the proper sacrifices were made, they took care of their followers. The rain god brought rain, the fertility god brought children, the green thumb god brought good crops, and the war god brought victory in battle. The ancients had a god for every need. If their god was not working for them, then they changed gods. If the neighboring tribe had better crops, then they had a better god. If the kingdom next door got more rain, then their god was better. They would not think of serving a god that could not deliver. What good is a god who does not do things for you?

The king challenges Shadrach, Meshach, and Abednego's God to a duel. "Your God will not rescue you; my god is better than yours." Like the child saying, "My daddy can beat up your daddy." This was a challenge with a furnace for the loser. But Shadrach, Meshach, and Abednego present a startling new concept of God and worship. The response of Daniel's three friends gives Nebuchadnezzar a dramatically new picture of God. "The God we serve is able to save us from it, and he will rescue us from your hand, O king. But even if he does not, we want you to know, O king, that we will not serve your gods or worship the image of gold you have set up" (verses 17, 18). In other words, "Our God can rescue us, but He is not a rabbit's foot for us to rub when we are in trouble. Our God is able to rescue us, but He may choose not to do so, and that will not change our commitment to Him."

To Nebuchadnezzar's way of thinking, the god that lost this duel was not worthy of worship, was not worthy to be a god at all. He was a loser god if he did not provide protection. If he does not provide rain, if he does not prevent the accident, if he does not provide children, if he does not get you a job, if he does not cure you of cancer, if he does not give you victory in battle, then who needs him! For Nebuchadnezzar, any god that didn't do his bidding was not worthy to be a god. But to Shadrach, Meshach, and Abednego, their God was more than a genie in a bottle of wishes or a Santa Claus in the sky.

Shadrach, Meshach, and Abednego's God was The God, the Creator God to be served and worshiped because He is God, not because He provides protection. He is to be loved for who He is, not what He can do for them. They were originally educated in the simple classrooms of Jerusalem. It was there that they first received an education that made them ten times wiser than the graduates from the University of Babylon. It was there, in Jerusalem, that they learned of a God who is not made in the image of man's wants. Theirs was no designer god built by man to please man and make him comfortable.

Christian education, of the Jerusalem kind, gives us a God to worship that is worthy of worship no matter what kind of conflicts we face. The golden statue of a secular education ignores the true God and fabricates gods of human wisdom that provide no moral base.

Ordinary men

Reserve Police Battalion 101 was based in Hamburg, Germany, but they were serving in Poland. This group was composed of mostly middle-aged family men of working and lower-middle-class backgrounds from the city of Hamburg. Considered too old to be of use to the German army, they had been drafted instead into the Order Police. They were raw recruits with no previous experience in German-occupied territory.

Education

On July 13, 1942, Reserve Police Battalion 101 was on the edge of the Polish city of Józefów. They were about to be instructed on their first major action. The village of Józefów was a typical Polish village of modest white houses with thatched straw roofs. Among its inhabitants were 1,800 Jews.

Early that morning, as the sun was just rising, the men of Reserve Police Battalion 101 climbed down from their trucks and assembled in a half-circle around their commander. They, rifles in hand, waited for instructions as to their task on this mystery mission. They were to listen to Major Wilhelm Trapp, a 53-year-old career policeman. He was to give them their assignment.

Major Trapp was pale and nervous, with choking voice and tears in his eyes he spoke. The battalion had to perform a frightfully unpleasant task, he said. The assignment was not to his liking; indeed, it was highly regrettable, but the orders came from the highest authorities.

The battalion had been ordered to round up Jews. The male Jews of working age were to be separated and taken to a work camp. The remaining Jews—the women, children, and elderly—were to be shot on the spot by the battalion. Having explained what their task was, Major Trapp made an offer: If any of the older men among them did not feel up to the task that lay before him, he could step out. Ten to twenty percent of the battalion stepped out, turned in their rifles and were told to await further assignment. Major Trapp complained about his orders and wept bitterly, but his men proceeded to carry out the battalion's task.

Search teams of 2, 3 and 4 went into the Jewish section of Józefów, and others guarded the streets leading to the marketplace. The Jews were rounded up and sent to the marketplace. A battalion physician explained precisely how they should shoot in order to bring immediate death. He outlined the upper contour of a human body on the ground and indicated precisely the point on which the fixed bayonet was to be placed as an aiming guide, just behind the head.

The young and healthy men were marched off to a labor camp, and the women, children and elderly were marched to the woods where they were forced to lie face down in a row, they were shot, and then more were marched in from the village square, and the same sequence of shooting proceeded.[2]

One thousand five hundred people were killed that day, July 13, 1942, in the little Polish village of Józefów. They were killed by "ordinary" men. *Ordinary Men* is the title of a book by Christopher Browning that relates this story.[3] Only 10 to 20 percent, when given a choice, refused to carry out the immoral assignment. Most who were given the option to refuse chose to follow along with the crowd.

These were ordinary men, men with wives and children. They had jobs in Hamburg. They were barbers, mechanics, and farmers. Some of them, no doubt, considered themselves Christians. Why did these "ordinary men" commit extraordinary horrors? There are several explanations and rationalizations, but their education had apparently not given them any moral backbone allowing them to stand against immoral orders. The god they worshiped was not the Creator God. No, they had a designer god, a god that was good for church and nice for an occasional prayer, but not one that could cause them to stand for principle on the plain of Dura.

A call to heroism

Is our God a designer god made in our image, responding like a genie in a bottle to our wants? Is He a god that only satisfies

73

our needs without crossing our desires? Is our God a designer god, fabricated with the clay of feelings, baked in the oven of our desires, fired in the kiln of our imagination? Such a concept of God is a heathen idea, no less heathen than the god of Nebuchadnezzar erected on the plain of Dura.

If our god makes no demands, asks no favors, and closes no doors on our worldly desires, then our god is a designer god, a heathen god and conditioned by culture. Just because we call him Jesus makes him no different from a golden statue on the plain of Dura, a lucky rabbit's foot, a charm, only to be used to approve what worldly desires demand.

Shadrach, Meshach, and Abednego's Jerusalem education stayed with them when they were led captive into Babylon. They didn't leave their convictions when they walked onto the plain of Dura. Let us not have our children worship at the feet of a worldly education, accepting the designer doctrines of a post-Christian culture fabricated in the New Age laboratories of a heathen society.

Babylon needs Shadrachs, Meshachs, and Abednegos. Not ordinary students but extraordinary men and women who will stand up on the plain of Dura when everyone else bows down. Young people who live with moral courage in an immoral world! Walker Percy warned in his book *The Second Coming* that it is possible to get all As and flunk at life.[4]

It will take more than academic intelligence and parental convictions to live a spiritual life in Babylon today. It will take more than cultural Adventism to be Christian in Babylon today. Nothing can hide the fact that the Christian religion is centered on the cross. Christians who claim Christ with no cross have not claimed Christ at all. We cannot expect God to do more for us than He did for Jesus, and He led Him to a cross. Christianity is a call to heroism. It is a counterculture movement that will not tolerate a designer god.

Fenton Forest

Once upon a time deep in Fenton Forest, so deep in the dark part of the woods that rarely did Freddy the Fox ever go there and never did Lightfoot the deer ever darken the forest floor there, back deep in the forest past Ivy Lane and Pine Nut street where there were no forest paths and no homes of any Fenton Forest folk, deep in the dark part of the forest that would frighten most anyone, right next to a very large knurled old oak tree, by some moss-covered stones, was a flower that bloomed.

She was a pretty flower, with waxy yellow petals and pale green stem; she lifted her head above the dark, dank forest floor and opened wide her pedals to the scarce light that filtered down through the trees to her place at the base of the old oak tree.

There she stood, a solitary spot of yellow, like a splash of paint, on the dark landscape of the primeval forest floor. She sent out her perfumed flower fragrance on light breezes, hoping that some bee who might have strayed from its flight path would follow the scent to her side.

There she grew, droplets of dew glistening from her canary-colored petals. Day after day she was there in the deepest, darkest part of Fenton Forest. Week after week, she was there in the obscure recesses of the forest; during the entire season of her life, she was there—blooming.

No errant bee traveler found her delightful nectar there by the big oak, no passing bird saw her splash of yellow, and no meandering forest inhabitant observed the glory she brought to her little dark glen.

The season of her life came to an end as her golden saffron petals faded onto the colorless mat of the forest floor to provide nutrients for a future flower generation.

The old oak said to her as she faded her last, "It was hardly worth it, was it—such color wasted in the deep darkness of the forest."

75

Education

She replied as she died there by the roots of the ancient oak, "I just bloom where I am planted, and God sees."

---

1. Richard Lovelace, "To Althea, from Prison," 1642, https://www.poetryfoundation.org/poems/44657/to-althea-from-prison.

2. "When Is Someone Accountable for Their Own Actions Who," HIST 338, Colorado State University, https://www.coursehero.com/file/p7fvlk8/When-is-someone-accountable-for-their-own-actions-Who-are-these-ordinary-men/.

3. Christopher R. Browning, *Ordinary Men: Reserve Police Battalion 101 and the Final Solution in Poland* (New York: HarperPerennial, 1992).

4. Walker Percy, *The Second Coming* (New York: Picador, 1980), 32, 93.

Eight

Education and Redemption

Ellen White summarizes the relationship between education and redemption in her book *Education*. "To restore in man the image of his Maker, to bring him back to the perfection in which he was created, to promote the development of body, mind, and soul, that the divine purpose in his creation might be realized—this was to be the work of redemption. This is the object of education, the great object of life."[1]

Institutional grace

How does one best communicate the story of redemption and the gift of free grace in an educational setting? The expressions "act naturally," "found missing," "plastic glasses," and "giant shrimp" are known as oxymorons—expressions that in their superficial or literal meaning are self-contradictory. Does the term "institutional grace" also fit that definition? Is it an oxymoron? Is it possible to communicate grace in an institution such as a church or school?

The nature of grace is accepting and forgiving, while the nature of an institution is to establish itself by using rules, policies, and regulations. Grace accepts you as you are, shortcomings and all, while an institution is more likely to accept you when you measure up.

The word *institution* comes from a root word that means "to stand" or "to establish." The institution is organized by people who "stand" for something and who wish to perpetuate their convictions. Therefore, they establish policies and standards. To ensure that their convictions persist into the future, they "institutionalize" their ideas. The result? Institutions develop church manuals, policy manuals, student handbooks, and education codes and teach those things and require certain behaviors. This institutional oversight brings us back to the question, Is *institutional grace* an oxymoron?

I heard a story about a woman who had a child out of wedlock, and the church extended grace by welcoming her into the church. They gave her a baby shower and helped her extensively as she cared for her newborn. The result? It all went so well that she had another child out of wedlock. When are we enablers, and when are we extending grace? Imagine Moses, the institutional leader, saying, "Lord, these children of Yours have built a golden calf. I think that this is a problem of environmental depravity caused by their poor home conditions in Egypt. They are not responsible for these actions." That was not the response of Moses or God. It was clear that the Israelites needed to learn a lot about the God who had redeemed them from Egypt; they needed a lot of education about God's grace and His law.

In the New Testament, church leaders sought to find the balance between the application of law and grace. These leaders were teaching the newly forming church about the true God and how He was redeeming humanity. "Some men came down from Judea to Antioch and were teaching the brothers: 'Unless you are circumcised, according to the custom taught by Moses, you cannot be saved' " (Acts 15:1).

They were educating the new believers that salvation required the performance of certain Jewish rites, such as circumcision. They wanted to make circumcision a requirement of being redeemed. "You can't abandon the rules given to us by Father Abraham!" they exclaimed. "This brought Paul and Barnabas into sharp dispute and debate with them. So, Paul and Barnabas were appointed . . . to go up to Jerusalem to see the apostles and elders about this question" (verse 2).

Individualism and conformity

We live in an age of individualism that generally thumbs its nose at institutional rules. The response to church and school is, "I am my own person, and you should not presume to restrict my liberty." We can learn something from Paul's response to the dispute in the early church. Why did Paul go to Jerusalem? It is because he cared about the community. The institution, the church, was important to him. What "the brethren" had to say mattered to Paul.

> When they came to Jerusalem, they were welcomed by the church and the apostles and elders, to whom they reported everything God had done through them.
> Then some of the believers who belonged to the party of the Pharisees stood up and said, "The Gentiles must be circumcised and required to obey the law of Moses" (verses 4, 5).

If you translated this into a contemporary setting, it might read, "Then some of the believers who belonged to the conservative party stood up and said, 'We must not allow anyone who eats meat, wears jewelry, or _____ to join the church.' " (I am sure you could fill in the blank from your experience.)

The demand for Gentile conformity was heard, and "the apostles and elders met to consider this question" (verse 6). I wish I could have listened in on this committee meeting of the apostles and elders. Considering the relationship between Jews and Gentiles during this time, it was no doubt a passionate discussion. The Jews regarded the Gentiles as heathens. According to Jewish law, you didn't marry them, you didn't eat with them, and you didn't enter their houses. Now all of these "heathen" were accepting Jesus and joining the church. I am sure the Jews who had been following God all along claimed that the standards were falling. They wanted to educate these new followers of Jesus in the rules of the Torah. In defending their views, they quoted the Old Testament rules about circumcision (see Genesis 17:9–14; Leviticus 12:3; Genesis 34:15).

"After much discussion, Peter got up and addressed them: 'Brothers, you know that some time ago God made a choice among you that the Gentiles might hear from my lips the message of the gospel and believe. God, who knows the heart, showed that he accepted them by giving the Holy Spirit to them, just as he did to us. He made no distinction between us and them, for he purified their hearts by faith. Now then, why do you try to test God by putting on the necks of the disciples a yoke that neither we nor our fathers have been able to bear? No! We believe it is through the grace of our Lord Jesus that we are saved, just as they are' " (Acts 15:7–11).

Thus, in the early development of the institutional church, Peter noted that God made no distinction between Gentile sinners and Jewish saints, pointing out that all live under grace. James summarizes the decision made at that first General Conference session.

When they finished, James spoke up: "Brothers, listen to me. Simon has described to us how God at first showed his concern by taking from the Gentiles a people for himself. . . .

"It is my judgment, therefore, that we should not make it difficult for the Gentiles who are turning to God" (verses 13–19).

Don't make it difficult

The basis of the decision was not a string of quotations from the Old Testament, proving the importance of circumcision. The Judaizers were doing that. They didn't decide to set up circumcision clinics in churches. The leaders didn't get out the policy book, the church manual, or the student handbook. James expressed what seemed to be the consensus of the group after their discussion. And that consensus was expressed in six words: "We should not make it difficult." Human institutions tend toward making things difficult, toward being exclusive. We like to belong to a privileged group and to be chosen for the platinum credit card and the first-class upgrade on an airplane flight. The party of the Pharisees wanted to use their "club" to elevate their exclusivity. Jesus came to teach us about what God is like, and He is not exclusive but desires all to receive redemption (see 1 Timothy 2:3, 4).

What does "not make it difficult" mean in an institution, in a church or school setting? It means rational rules mediated by relationships. If institutional rules are understandable and explainable to a reasonable person, then they are "not difficult"! Notice, I said, "a reasonable person." (I know that churches and schools don't always deal with reasonable persons.) Adventist educational institutions are presented with a complicated task. On the one hand, the gospel is free, and the story of salvation is taught as not being behavior dependent. On the other hand, this task is pursued in a social setting that requires a rather long list of behavioral standards and rules.

Rule categories

Discipline is necessary for every institution, including schools and churches. No group can achieve community unless it holds some things in common. The very definition of *community* is to hold some things in common, and that means rules and law, which require discipline. But the human inclination is to apply *punishment,* not *discipline.* Discipline is redemptive, whereas punishment is punitive. In a disciplined community, the members express responsibility for one another by making sure that correction is applied with grace. If we look at different categories of rules, it will help institutions "not make it difficult" for students and church members. Dividing rules into categories may help.

First, some behavior standards are integral to doctrinal beliefs, integral to the community's very existence. Without these laws or rules, the community does not hold anything in common and is not a community at all. The Ten Commandments and the twenty-eight fundamental beliefs would fall into this category. They are an expression of fundamental church teachings and are supported by Scripture, providing the community with its core identity. These rules are not negotiable.

Second, some behavior standards grow out of our religious, cultural heritage. Among other things, these include conservative dress standards and Sabbath church attendance. We refrain from or embrace these items because they form a part of our image—this is who we are. They are part of our religious tradition. These rules or policies reflect our corporate culture and how we wish to represent ourselves. We don't exclude people from the church, nor do we make judgments about them if they don't follow these rules.

Third, some behavior policies are necessary rules of engagement for situations when adolescents and adults are in close proximity. These include such things as where you can park your car and, for a school, such regulations as storing cell phones during class and not eating in the library.

To create rational regulations, we need to understand these categories of rules. We must not seek to place heavy moral implications on the transgression of behavior standards that are merely institutional or cultural norms.

Of course, even when administrators feel they have a good

rationale for a rule, students and parents may not agree. So, in the end, it is the relationship that balances law and grace. The Old Testament provides us with a perfect illustration. The Shekinah glory, or presence of God, resided in the mercy seat above the tablets of the law. It was there that mercy and law joined. The presence of God brought them together. In New Testament times, Jesus showed us through His life and teachings how to combine law and grace. He died to uphold the law *and* to give us grace.

In the setting of Christian education, we have incarnational teachers, deans, and administrators who combine law and grace in their lives. They model living the rules and loving the students. The institution does not communicate grace by either throwing out the rules or making them innocuous. It communicates grace by having grace-filled people, those who have experienced the gospel in their own lives, mediate the rules of institutional life. Pastors, faculty, and staff first must melt students with their love before they can mold their opinions. Too often, we seek to mold their opinion before we melt them— and they rebel. Through loving relationships, we can unite grace and law. The following chart illustrates the grace-full school:

Issue	Non-Grace Orientation	Grace Orientation
School atmosphere	Cold and suspicious	Friendly and accepting
Principal	Warden	Helper
Teachers	Police	Mentors
Employees	Treated with suspicion	Treated with trust
Dormitory	Prison	Home
Deans	Parole officers	Friends
Acceptance policies	Open to the perfect	Open to the teachable
Student handbook	What you cannot do	What you do not want to do

Questions	Do not ask	Freedom to ask
Obedience	From fear	From love
Sin	Breaking the rules	Breaking the relationship
Second Coming	Fear	Joy
Faith	Leap in the dark	Leap into light
God	Judge to appease	Father to love
Law	Restrictive instruction	Loving guidelines

At the beginning of this chapter, we used Moses as an illustration of someone who would not ignore the sins of the Israelites when they worshiped a golden calf. He administered some severe punishment. But God suggested to Moses, "I have seen these people, . . . and they are a stiff-necked people. Now leave me alone so that my anger may burn against them and that I may destroy them. Then I will make you into a great nation" (Exodus 32:9, 10). Then Moses manifested the love of a true leader. He went back to the Lord and said, "Oh, what a great sin these people have committed! They have made themselves gods of gold. But now, please forgive their sin—but if not, then blot me out of the book you have written" (verse 31).

Moses mediated the law with such love that he was willing to relinquish his salvation for the people he served. That kind of love will always communicate grace, even in an institutional setting with many rules.

So is institutional grace an oxymoron? No, unless the people of the institution are not incarnational representatives of Jesus and His love. When pastors, administrators, and teachers experience God's love and His unconditional acceptance, there will be institutional grace, and it will not be an oxymoron.

Fenton Forest

Many years ago, in Fenton Forest, a decision had been made

that all the forest folks would get a free lunch. It was felt that this would decrease the high level of poverty and assure a stable forest environment. For a few years, it seemed to work well, and there was a higher standard of living in the forest; and with no need to compete over the food supply, the folks got along better. Fenton Forest became a lovely place to live.

Sometime after the free-lunch policy went into effect, a group began to question the policy. It had been many years since it was instituted, and they, in their careful study of economics, concluded that there was no such thing as a free lunch. They began to express doubts about the generosity of the one who provided it and his ability to keep paying for it.

It was the conviction of this group that their economic and forest conditions would improve if each person paid for their own lunch. They said it would bring more money into the local forest economy, and the result would be a better forest. Besides, how did they know how long their benefactor would be able to continue providing the free lunch?

They called those who wanted a free lunch *freeloaders*—folk who were not contributing to the forest economy. They ignored the fact that those on the free-lunch program were working as hard as they, and in some cases, a bit harder. They rallied around the slogan "There is no such thing as a free lunch!"

Then one day, the one who had made the decision concerning the free-lunch program and who had also paid for free lunches came and found that His generous provisions had not been accepted or appreciated by some. He asked them why, but they were speechless. And so he cast them out into outer darkness, where there was weeping and gnashing of teeth.

---

1. Ellen G. White, *Education* (Mountain View, CA: Pacific Press®, 1903), 15, 16.

Nine

The Church
and Education

I was shocked, confused, bewildered
As I entered Heaven's door,
Not by the beauty of it all,
Nor the lights or its decor.

But it was the folks in Heaven
Who made me sputter and gasp—
The thieves, the liars, the sinners,
The alcoholics and the trash.

There stood the kid from seventh grade
Who swiped my lunch money twice.
Next to him was my old neighbor
Who never said anything nice.

Bob, who I always thought
Was rotting away in hell,
Was sitting pretty on cloud nine,
Looking incredibly well.

I nudged Jesus, "What's the deal?
I would love to hear Your take.
How'd all these sinners get up here?
God must've made a mistake.

"And why is everyone so quiet,
So somber—give me a clue."
"Hush, child," He said,
"they're all in shock.
No one thought they'd be seeing you."[1]

Comparing ourselves

I was walking along the street back to my car in downtown Chattanooga after a Rotary meeting. A large black man approached me, and my first thought was, *He is a panhandler and is going to ask me for money.* Imagine my surprise when he simply asked, "Are you saved?"

I had misjudged him. It is this type of misjudgment that destroys community and undermines the church. We think, *They are not like us; they are a different color; they are not dressed like we are,* and we find false security in a world that is just like us. But our world is full of diversity, and as Christians, we recognize everyone as being a part of the family of God.

This tendency to assess, or judge, people is selfishness. It is as if we place everyone on a scale and seek to determine where they are in relationship to our pecking order. How much money do they make? What kind of car do they drive? How do they dress? Paul addressed this attitude in the Corinthian church: "They are only comparing themselves with each other, using themselves as the standard of measurement. How ignorant!" (2 Corinthians 10:12, NLT).

Comparing ourselves with others doesn't build community. God lives in community—God the Father, God the Son, and God the Holy Spirit have been in community for eternity. In heavenly council, they decided to expand that community to include humanity. "So, God created human beings in his own image. In the image of God he created them, male and female he created them" (Genesis 1:27, NLT).

God loves community

One thing that being created in the image of God means is to be in community. After God created each day, He saw "that it was good" (verse 18, NLT). However, after God created Adam, there was one thing that was not good. "The LORD God said, 'It is not good for the man to be alone. I will make a helper who is just right for him' " (Genesis 2:18, NLT).

God has never been alone. He has lived throughout all eternity in the community of the Trinity, and we were created for community, to live in loving unity with one another. A loving solitary God is impossible, for love is always looking outside of itself. Love is unfulfilled if there is no object of that love. Creation is simply the extension of the love that is intrinsic to the Trinity, a community that has existed for all time in an atmosphere of love.

What is your church like? What kind of education does your church provide? Is it a loving community where people feel accepted? Do visitors feel like they are home when they come into your church? Is it a place where any question can be asked without being judged? If the church is to be a place of education (we do have Sabbath Schools), then questions should be welcome. "Do not judge others, and you will not be judged. For you will be treated as you treat others. The standard you use in judging is the standard by which you will be judged" (Matthew 7:1, 2, NLT).

What does the average American think of church? The Gallup organization and the Princeton Religious Research Center did research on the unchurched.[2] Many people want religion but not organized religion. Many people want spirituality but not church. As one person said, "Half the people who go to church are hypocrites. They go because it's the thing to do, not because they believe. It's a status thing. They think, 'I went to church today, so I'm a good person.' I can pray and believe in my own way."[3] This is not exactly a new thought, though. John Heywood, who lived in the sixteenth century, wrote, "*The neer to the church, the further from God.*"[4]

The founders of our church were not enthusiastic about "church" or "organized religion," for they had been rather arbitrarily expelled from their churches. They had not been given an opportunity to give a Bible answer for their newfound faith. They had been silenced and ejected from churches for their belief in the soon return of Jesus. Understandably, there was a lingering bad taste in their mouths for organized religion.[5] Those early Millerite attitudes would find acceptance today in our society where people want spirituality but not religion, Jesus but not denomination.

In the Valuegenesis study[6] of Seventh-day Adventist young people, a measurement of congregational effectiveness factors found that 81 percent of academy-aged students experienced the teaching of Adventist standards in their schools and churches. However, only 35 percent indicated that the church has a warm climate, and only 27 percent indicated that they often experience caring adults. Those statistics need to be reversed. For too many church members, all that Seventh-day Adventism stands for is some rather peculiar behavior characteristic rather than the love of God manifest in the community of the church. The early church demonstrated the unity and community of God.

In the early church, "all the believers were together and had everything in common. They sold property and possessions to give to anyone who had need" (Acts 2:44, 45, TNIV). We were created for community and for fellowship with God. But the church is threatened by individualism. The focus of our postmodern society is on the individual and whatever he or she wants.

This development places us in danger of slipping into enclaves of isolation on Facebook and Snapchat with our electronic devices, listening only to those we agree with, and judging those we don't. There is a cocooning of society as people separate into isolated, polarized groups, electronically connected by uniform beliefs, color, country, or prejudice.

In the book *Habits of the Heart*, Robert Bellah spoke of community as a useful contrast term to an alienating individualism. "Talk radio . . . mobilizes private opinion, not public opinion, and trades on anxiety, anger, and distrust, all of which are deadly to civic culture."[7]

I heard of a church once that was polarized over some theological issues, and one couple that identified with one of the polarities typically sat in a specific pew in church. The pastoral staff became aware of the need for more open areas for positioning of wheelchairs and, not thinking of who usually sat there, decided to cut off a pew to make room for a wheelchair. Wouldn't you know, they cut off the pew where this couple sat. The rumor went around that the pastoral staff was sending a message that this couple wasn't wanted in the church.

Community and individualism

Have you ever been in a church where community trust broke down? People gather in clusters. People leave quickly after church. People avoid certain people. Potlucks become a problem. A lot of energy is spent on nonproductive activities. People call people and talk about people. As one person said, "Christians don't gossip. They just share prayer requests!"[8]

In organizations, it has been observed that the first generation focuses on mission, the second generation focuses on doctrine, and the third generation focuses on bureaucracy. Where is our church? Is it birds of a feather flocking together for mutual preening? Is it simply to be with people who eat like we do, live like we do, believe like we do, and are compatible with us? Or is it a community that lives as one in unity, as Jesus asked in John 17:21, "so that the world will believe you sent me" (NLT)? All churches provide an education; the question is, what kind of education does your church provide?

A quotation often attributed to George Eliot says, "Oh, the inexpressible comfort of feeling safe with a person; having neither to weigh thoughts nor measure words, but to pour them all out, just as they are, chaff and grain together, knowing that a faithful hand will take and sift them, keep what is worth keeping, and then, with the breath of kindness, blow the rest away."

We will not continue believing the teachings of Jesus that don't touch the significant meanings in our lives. We can maintain the teaching of the church for a generation or two, but in the long run, that which does not affect our lives will disappear from our beliefs. We pass on from one generation to another the gospel and the teachings of Jesus, not by doctrinal formulations, not by creedal statements, but by experiencing them for ourselves. The church should then be the kind of community that is Jesus in action, a little heaven on earth, a living expression of Jesus' description of the Christian community as He presented it in the Sermon on the Mount (see Matthew 5–7).

Sometimes I think of the church like the experience of the mouse I found in our garage. I heard this scraping sound as I was getting into the car to go to work. I looked around, and there was the cat's bowl, scooting along the floor. I looked more closely and determined that a mouse had trapped itself under the cat's bowl. It was safe from the cat but was not living much of a life. Some have experienced the church as a trap rather than finding the freedom of the gospel there. We must not isolate ourselves from others in individual cocoons of safety. Our churches must be more engaged in the community and not separate ourselves from the world as the remnant waiting for the Lord to come and rescue us. The only safety for the church is living as God created us—for community.

The difference between heaven and hell

There is a story told of a man who died and went to heaven. (Like the story of the rich man and Lazarus, this story is a parable.) When he arrived at the pearly gates, he met Saint Peter, who looked over his credentials and told him that he could come into heaven.

The man said, "I think I would appreciate heaven more if I could first see what hell is like. I would like to go to hell."

Saint Peter tried to discourage him from such a trip, but the man insisted, and so Saint Peter directed an angel to accompany him to hell. He went with his angel guide down a long staircase to hell. When they arrived, the man was astonished at how beautiful it was. There were swans on lakes, green fields, and everything was like what he had imagined the Garden of Eden looked like. He looked at the angel guide, and the angel, understanding his confusion, said, "Just wait." Then he saw a long building, and in the building were the residents of hell. He entered the building, and there was a table in the building around which sat all the residents of hell, and on the table was a feast fit for a king. All the most luxurious food imaginable was on the table for the residents of hell. But as the man looked closer, he noted that all the residents of hell were starving to death; they were emaciated and in great pain. The man looked to the angel guide, and the angel said that all the residents of hell had their arms in splints and couldn't get the food to their mouths.

"Oh, now I understand why hell is so terrible," the man said. "I know I will appreciate heaven more; please, take me out of this dreadful place and back up to heaven."

So the angel guide took him back to heaven, and they went

through the pearly gates. Heaven looked for all the world like hell. There were the swans on the lakes and the beautiful green fields. Then the man went into a building in heaven that looked like the one he saw in hell, and in it, the residents of heaven were seated around a long table that was piled high with the bountiful banquet that was exactly like the one the man had seen in hell. As he looked closer, he noticed that all the residents of heaven also had their arms in splints and couldn't feed themselves, but they were all laughing and enjoying the food. The man turned to the angel guide and said, "I don't understand."

The angel guide said, "Oh, the only difference between heaven and hell is that in heaven, people feed each other."

And that is the only difference between heaven and hell. In hell, each person is so self-focused that they are in a black hole of selfishness, whereas in heaven, everyone loves one another, and they feed each other. Selfishness, the core of all sin, is a black hole of internal focus where all we think of is ourselves. Love is the core of all community as we give ourselves to others. Churches are schools where we learn to build community and make them a little heaven on earth, where people feel safe at home and yearn for their heavenly home.

---

1. "Best Poem in the World," Meme, accessed January 28, 2020, https://me.me/i/ap-best-poem-in-the-world-i-was-shocked-confused-6394792.

2. *A Summary of Qualitative Research of the Unchurched* (Religion in American Life, 1982), 7.

3. *Summary of Qualitative Research*, 7.

4. Julian Sharman, ed., *The Proverbs of John Heywood. Being the "Proverbes" of That Author Printed 1546* (London, 1874), 35; italics in original.

5. Leroy Edwin Froom, *Movement of Destiny* (Washington, DC: Review and Herald®, 1971), 133.

6. V. Bailey Gillespie et al., *Valuegenesis—Ten Years Later: A Study of Two Generations* (Riverside, CA: Hancock Center, 2004).

7. Robert Bellah et al., *Habits of the Heart: Individualism and Commitment in American Life* (Berkeley, CA: University of California Press, 2008), xxiii.

8. Michael P. Green, ed., *Illustrations for Biblical Preaching* (Grand Rapids, MI: Baker Book House, 1989), s.v. "Gossip."

Ten

Education in Arts and Sciences

If you had lived in Zurich in 1524, you might have had a surprise as you arrived at church. You would have found all the pictures removed from the church, along with relics, altars, candles, and ornaments. The walls of the church would have been whitewashed, and there would be no music during the worship service. These reforms were the result of Ulrich Zwingli's ministry in Zurich and his effort to remove from worship any association with the Roman Catholic Church.

When organs were destroyed, it was not so much an aversion to the instrument as a rejection of the high church liturgy that they represented. Art and music originally designed to draw congregants to God had become objects of worship themselves, and Zwingli sought to bring worshipers back to the plain Word of God. Certainly, the Protestant Reformation and Martin Luther employed music in worship, and even Calvin, who would not use the organ, used the singing of psalms to great effect.[1] His music would not have been called "Geneva jigs"[2] unless there was some artistic innovation.

The Christian church has, through the ages, swung from the one extreme where art, symbols, and images are worshiped to the other extreme of the total elimination of artful representations of religious ideas. Some would blame Christianity for the destruction of much art, but when the truth was distorted by art, the Reformation required elimination of that art, in much the same way the elimination of Baal worship in the Old Testament required cutting down the sacred groves of trees even though those reformers were not opposed to trees.[3]

The word *worship* is derived from the Old English, meaning "to give, at its simplest, worth to something."[4] We were created to worship, and if our worship is not focused on God, it will be focused on something else. It might be giving worth to a hobby, a person, a job, children, science, art, or any number of things to which our actions ascribe worth. Because of this danger, what foundation can we lay for education in the arts and sciences in the Christian life?

Order out of chaos

"In the beginning God created the heaven and the earth. And the earth was without form, and void" (Genesis 1:1, KJV). The Creator took that which was without form, took that which had no coherence, and brought order out of chaos. And humankind, created in the image of God, has a part to play: "The LORD God took the man and put him in the Garden of Eden to work it, and take care of it" (Genesis 2:15).

God blessed Adam and Eve and gave them dominion. Like their heavenly Father, they sought to bring order out of chaos as they applied dominion over the earth. In the same way, teachers educate students, seeking to bring understanding in the sciences and inspiration in the beauty of art and music.

My wife is living up to the image of God as she seeks to bring order out of the chaos of my closet. Humankind, created in the image of God, seeks to bring form out of the formless, order from chaos. The Christian expresses being a child of God by creating, like his or her Father. The artist brings from the formless cedar, oak, lead, and gold an organ, and the musician uses it to produce majestic music. For the teacher of science, it may be the formless confusion that atheistic science uses to explain human origins with billions of years and the random motion of atoms and molecules. For the teachers of science, art, and music, it is eminently Christian to be creative with the formless. It is following in the Creator's footsteps.

Art and music feed the soul

If any of us were placed in the jungle, we would immediately seek to adapt to our environment. We would first try to provide for our shelter and food. When those needs were satisfied, we might pick a flower for the shelter and maybe cut down some bamboo to make a flute. It is part of the image of God placed within us to go beyond securing our physical being to the adventure of aesthetic creation.

> If of thy mortal goods thou art bereft,
> And from thy slender store two loaves alone to thee are left,
> Sell one, and with the dole
> Buy hyacinths to feed thy soul.[5]

Christians have a special reason to buy hyacinths to feed the soul, to take the world around them and bring order out of it. For in so doing, they are exercising the *imago Dei*, the image of God, and aiding students in seeing God in His creation and being God's children by being creative.

During most of the history of Christianity, the general population was illiterate, and for that reason, art and music were used to tell Bible stories. A twelfth-century bishop wrote to an artist: "Adorning the ceiling and walls with varied work and diverse colors, you have in some way exposed to the eyes of the faithful the Paradise of God, decorated with innumerable flowers. You have succeeded in letting the Creator be praised in creation and in showing God to be admirable in his work."[6] Today,

Christians continue to give praise to God and imitate the heavenly Father by creating music, art, and instruments. Creating order where there was disorder.

God loves beauty

The growth of scientific thought came from those seeking to understand God's creation, but scientific endeavor today, with its atheistic materialist presuppositions, is driven by those who exclude God from the equation. As Peter says, "They conveniently forget that long ago all the galaxies and this very planet were brought into existence out of watery chaos by God's word" (2 Peter 3:5, *The Message*).

Science education that excludes the Creator results in students left without a moral foundation for life. The results are made clear in Paul's writing to the Romans. "But God's angry displeasure erupts as acts of human mistrust and wrongdoing and lying accumulate, as people try to put a shroud over truth. But the basic reality of God is plain enough. Open your eyes and there it is! By taking a long and thoughtful look at what God has created, people have always been able to see what their eyes as such can't see: eternal power, for instance, and the mystery of his divine being. So nobody has a good excuse" (Romans 1:18–20, *The Message*).

What basis is there for decisions with moral consequences if the only standard is the survival of the fittest? That selfish evolutionary principle gives priority to the powerful, but Jesus came to uplift the downtrodden.

> "The Spirit of the Lord is on me,
>   because he has anointed me
>   to preach good news to the poor.
> He has sent me to proclaim freedom for the prisoners
>   and recovery of sight for the blind,
> to release the oppressed" (Luke 4:18).

Education in Arts and Sciences

The design we see in nature points to an artistic Creator Designer expressing the glory and beauty of God. The Christian teacher of science and art, with a biblical worldview, teaches from the foundational perspective of God's creation. This education draws a distinction between the foolishness of false wisdom that excludes acknowledging the Creator and the beauty of fearing God and embracing the Creator Designer.

The educational value of art and music

Some might say that a work of art or music has no use; it is not practical. What do you do with it? They would buy no hyacinths, only bread. But it is this aspect of art, its uselessness from a utilitarian standpoint, that makes it so useful. For it calls us from utilitarianism, where everything must be used for something. It calls us from materialism, where the focus is on getting a return on your investment. It calls us in symbols to reach beyond the visible to the invisible God. The creation of art and music gives form to our feeling, touching the untouchable like an MRI scan pictures the body's internal organs. Similarly, art and music photograph our spirits, the thoughts and feelings that stir deep within us. Unfortunately, in the secular education of public institutions where a Creator God is excluded, music, art, and science have little moral foundation and frequently expose the spirit of evil and sin that is pervasive in society's perversion of God's creation.

There are occasions when listening to a piece of music gives you chills. Have you ever been watching a movie during some exciting part and, not wanting to get too involved in the drama, turned off the sound? It lowers the dramatic effect tenfold. When I listen to Vaughan Williams's "Serenade to Music," I remember singing it in college, and I sing along. It calls up memories. It touches the untouchable, the ineffable.

Education must do more than ask significant questions and

provide satisfying answers. Education must do more than provide fellowship. Education must do more than offer advice for ethical living. The goal of education is not merely to convince people intellectually of the value of religion but to help them feel this value in the depths of their being.[7]

Worship is an educational art form, and our music is the brush with which we apply the paint of religious faith to our innermost spirit. The music is not to provide mood music. It is not to fill in empty spaces in a worship service. It is to assist us in expressing the inexpressible. Music is an act of worship that, as Samuel Mitter has said, is "the projection in a specific place at a specific time of what the worshippers believe to be the nature of ultimate reality."[8]

Some would discount the educational value of corporate worship, preferring the primacy of individual meditation. However, the individual endeavor provides no broader reach than our personal sphere. In corporate worship, we join hands as it were, and our mutual expression is greater than the sum of its parts. The primary way we join hands in our worship is through musical expression. The focus of worship is on the Word, the Word that was made flesh, the factual expression of the will of God through His Word. This Word must always be sovereign, but it must also reach deeply into our soul, touching our hearts and feelings. In this regard, music and the arts educate us in ways that sermons do not.

Art and music must stand in relation to Christian worship as an adjective, not as a noun. In Christianity, the integrity of the aesthetic language must come from theology. Nevertheless, there is a close relationship between the content of our lives and our music and art. There is a close relationship between our moral behavior and our music and art.[9]

Amos expressed God's concern about music divorced from behavior, the aesthetic experience separated from living:

"Away with the noise of your songs!
    I will not listen to the music of your harps.
But let justice roll on like a river,
    righteousness like a never-failing stream" (Amos 5:23, 24).

Music and art can be a veneer covering a weakness in spiritual life. Aesthetic experience can be sought as an end rather than a means to the end of glorifying God. Offerings to God that do not include the heart, that do not include justice and righteousness, are deceitful and may lull the worshiper into a false sense of security. One can be moved by music, but until one is moved to action in one's life, the sweet sounds are no better than drugs or a narcotic escape into self.

Fenton Forest

Once upon a time in Fenton Forest, Freddy the Fox was awakened by the loud singing of Jennifer Jay. It seems that Jennifer had found a secret store of Scamper the Squirrel's nuts close to Freddie's den. She was raiding the nuts and singing at the top of her lungs. Well, needless to say, Freddy was not too overjoyed at being wakened so early by Jennifer's singing.

"Would you quiet down!" Freddy cried out of his den door at Jennifer in the nearby tree. "Some civilized folk do like to sleep in the morning."

Jennifer paid no mind to Freddy—she rarely did—and she continued to sing lustily as she dug more deeply into Scamper's store of nuts.

"I know why you sing like that!" Freddy shouted. "The sound of your singing kills the worms in those nuts."

"You just don't appreciate good music!" Jennifer shouted back.

The argument was getting well underway when Wise Old Owl happened by and stopped to see what all the commotion was about.

Education

"Freddy doesn't like to hear the happy sounds of someone else's good fortune," Jennifer reported to Wise Old Owl.

Just then, off in the distance, there sounded a long clear blast of a horn.

"Now, that is another beautiful sound," Jennifer Jay said, pausing to listen to the mellow tones drift across the forest community.

"That sound is even more terrible than your singing!" said Freddy as he raced off up the hill.

"Where is he going so fast?" Jennifer asked Wise Old Owl.

"The sound of the fox hunt is not a beautiful sound to Freddy," said Wise Old Owl, who then reflected, "One's experience brings meaning to the sounds and the music you hear."

---

1. "And thus there is a great difference between the music that is made to entertain people at home and at table, and the Psalms which are sung in church, in the presence of God and His angels." From Calvin's Preface to the *Genevan Psalter* of 1543.

2. "Calvin and Geneva Jigs: Discussion in 'Semper Reformanda' started by Cajun Huguenot, Jan 10, 2006," Christian Forums, https://www.christianforums.com/threads/calvin-and-geneva-jigs.2506868/.

3. Francis A. Schaeffer, *How Should We Then Live* (Old Tappan, NJ: Fleming H. Revell, 1976), 89.

4. Wikipedia, s.v. "Worship," last modified September 3, 2019, 15:33, https://en.wikipedia.org/wiki/Worship.

5. Moslih Eddin Saadi, "Hyacinths to Feed Thy Soul," *The Best Loved Poems of the American People*, ed. Hazel Felleman (New York: Doubleday, 1936), 78.

6. Jacques Barzun, *The Use and Abuse of Art* (Princeton, NJ: Princeton University Press, 1974), 32.

7. Paul Hoon, *The Integrity of Worship: Ecumenical and Pastoral Studies in Liturgical Theology* (Nashville, TN: Abingdon Press, 1978), 200.

8. Hoon, *Integrity of Worship*, 41.

9. Hoon, *Integrity of Worship*, chapter 6.

Eleven

The Christian and Work

I recently retired and found that the transition from a full-time job to a part-time job (my wife thinks I have not retired) is challenging. Going from having a long "to-do" list involving multiple people to working alone in a home office is a significant change. It is nice to set my own schedule, but I miss the consistency of regular work hours and the fellowship with other employees. I knew one man who kept his routine when he retired. He would get up at the same time, dress in a business suit, and then go to a different room in his house, where he worked. He just kept his routine.

"To retire" typically means to cease work, but to no longer exercise the brain and the body makes them weak. Frailty is not a necessary consequence of getting old. Frailty comes to those who in retirement cease activity, for their brains and for their bodies. It is a false goal to look forward to retirement if retirement means to no longer work.

A definition of *work*
When we use the expression "it works," we mean that it is not broken, it does what it is supposed to do. It is also true of

people. They work when they are not broken. They may work at a hobby or a part-time job, but the meaning we find in life comes from making a contribution through work. Those who use retirement for sitting in a rocking chair and vegetating before the television will feel no fulfillment and will not live long. Retirement does not mean no work because "retirement from work has depressed many a man and hastened his death."[1] It is a vision of productive goals that keeps folks looking forward to tomorrow. My ninety-nine-year-old mother-in-law still likes to work by passing out tracts to people who visit her in the assisted living facility.

People frequently ask me, "How do you like retirement?" I hear them implying that I am no longer working, and so I am quick to tell them about all the work that I am doing in "retirement." "Anyone who stops learning is old, whether at twenty or eighty. Anyone who keeps learning stays young."[2] Lifelong learning is continued intellectual growth. This important and ongoing aspect of education provides the tools to grow intellectually for a person's entire life. There is no retirement for the growing the mind.

The word *labor* in the European languages creates a picture of compulsion or torment. The word is used to describe the pain in giving birth to a child, as "she is in labor." The French word *travail* and Spanish *trabajo* are both translated "work" as the English equivalent and are derived from the Latin *trepaliare*— to torture, to inflict suffering or agony. However, these images are not a picture of work that inspires!

To clarify the matter, we need to use the word *vocation*, not *work*. *Vocation* suggests a calling, a calling that one follows in life and not just a job that one must do to earn a living. When one ceases a particular job that is one expression of their vocation (in other words, they retire from that job), then they assume another responsibility that is a different expression of their calling. You never retire from a calling, or vocation. In many cases, that continuation of employment may be in a volunteer, non-remunerated capacity, but it is still an expression of vocation. It is like the advice I used to give college students, suggesting that they find a career they love, and they will never have to work a day in their lives.[3] Fulfilling one's calling does not feel like work, or travail. It is simply an outgrowth of a life seeking to use God-given gifts to serve others. You never retire from a vocation or calling. It is a lifelong pursuit to make an impact on the world, to change the world. Jason D. Stevens touches on this theme in his blog post "Vocation and the Apocalypse: McCarthy's *The Road*." "I ask students what makes the man's choice to live more than just fear of death or survival instinct. The answer is vocation: the man's sense of purpose elevates his choice to live from mere animal survival (cannibalistic gangs choose "life") to something genuinely human."[4]

The importance of work

Paul speaks of the importance of work, even suggesting that slaves serve their masters as they would serve Christ Himself. He says, "Work with enthusiasm, as though you were working for the Lord rather than for people" (Ephesians 6:7, NLT). To the Thessalonians, he says that those who do not work should not get to eat (2 Thessalonians 3:10).

Education itself is work; it is the work of solidifying a calling. Christian education is the process of leading the young to find a fulfilling vocation, a calling that gives them meaning as well as the opportunity to be of service to humanity. I would tell the freshmen students when they first came to Southern Adventist University that getting an education is your job; it is your work. The first thing you must do is show up for work. If you are not spending eight hours a day at work, you are not doing your job. You can be fired from this job of getting an education. Universities call it academic dismissal. The educational endeavor is about working your mind. As Ellen White says, "Every human being, created in the image of God, is endowed with a power akin to that of the Creator—individuality, power to think and to do. . . . It is the work of true education to develop this power, to train the youth to be thinkers, and not mere reflectors of other men's thought."[5]

Training thinkers

To become "thinkers, and not mere reflectors of other men's thought" demands an environment of safety where the young person can test thoughts in an atmosphere of academic freedom. In the secular university, academic freedom is claimed as the holy grail, and social restrictions of politically correct speech proscribe the thoughts of student and teacher alike, about as tightly as many denominationally sponsored schools.

Of course, there are boundaries to the conversations, but those who are not intimate participants must not, because they hear snippets of the conversation, jump to unwarranted conclusions about the faith of the communicators. There must be trust between constituent, faculty, staff, administration, and board of trustees. Education is not simply to accumulate certain facts about world history, chemistry, biology, religion, philosophy, mathematics, and computer science. Education is not just for the purpose of getting a job and becoming a cog in a capitalist economy, pursuing power and money. Christian education is to transform the thinking and character of the student.

Albert Meyer says, "Education is a conversation between the older and younger generations on what is important."[6] Higher education is a place for meaningful conversations between the older and the younger generation of Seventh-day Adventists. It is a place for having a conversation, secure in the knowledge that through mutual love and trust, we take each other's words as a sacred trust and sift out the chaff while holding firm to the wheat. In this relationship of mutual trust, the student has the freedom to test thoughts, and expressed thoughts that find no home in the community die a natural death. There should be no conspiracy theorists manufacturing, with the words of professor or student, a complex chain of accusations meant to trap people in dungeons of rumor to be published on a dissident website.

When I had doubts about something, my father used to say, "Doubt your doubts and believe your beliefs." Doubt is natural. Students should be encouraged to question things, for doing so is the prelude to knowledge. Colleges and universities do not provide all of the answers. A good education encourages students to ask hard questions and look at things from a variety of viewpoints. The faculty and staff will provide mentors as role models on how to relate to doubts and life in general. The good news of God's acceptance creates a nonthreatening atmosphere for educational conversations.

Ellen White says, "Ignorance is not acceptable to God, and is unfavorable for the doing of his work."[7] She even goes so far as to say that "ignorance is a crime when light and knowledge can be obtained."[8] Educational institutions do not exist to clone the past or protect the status quo. Our Lord died on the cross to protect our freedom, and we dishonor Him when our view of education is indoctrination rather than conversation, brainwashing rather than dialogue.

You cannot learn a skill in any school that will carry you through your entire life. Change in the workplace comes too rapidly. Education is not so much to learn a trade as it is to learn how to live life. Education is not filling the mind with lots of facts; it is lighting the fire of curiosity about the world and life. You cannot learn a bit of knowledge in school that will carry you through life. Instead, the work of the student is to learn how to learn, to learn how to continually adapt to changing time, to be a lifelong learner.

Aldous Huxley's dystopian novel *Brave New World* describes a world in the year 2540 where humans are cloned to perform jobs like machines are designed to do a task, resulting in the loss of morals and humanity.[9] We are many years from 2540, but the linking of artificial intelligence with machines points to a future in which work is more and more of the mind and less and less about physical abilities. This all points to the importance of an education that guides the young to a vocation of service with the moral underpinnings of a biblical foundation. Wisdom without a biblical foundation is prone to result in a dystopian society that is the opposite of God's plan for His kingdom on earth. "The fear of the Lord is the beginning of wisdom; all who follow his precepts have good understanding. To him belongs eternal praise" (Psalm 111:10).

Fenton Forest

Once upon a time in Fenton Forest, Freddy the Fox and Gruff the Bear got to talking about how nice it would be to have fresh food from a garden. The subject came up because Freddy received a seed catalog in the mail, and it had a lot of color pictures of mouthwatering fruits and vegetables. Just looking at the pictures made them hungry. As they talked about it, they really got excited. "We could each have a garden, and what we didn't use ourselves, we could sell!" said Gruff.

"Good idea!" Freddy replied, "People always want fresh carrots, tomatoes, and watermelons, and I always want more money."

"We could build a fruit-and-vegetable stand on Ivy Lane just across from Scamper's Nut Hut!" Gruff growled. Gruff always growled when he got excited.

Freddy added, "If Scamper the Squirrel can make some money selling nuts at the Nut Hut, why can't we make money with a fruit-and-vegetable stand?" It all looked so easy that they both decided to go ahead with their plans and each plant a garden.

Now Freddy was never one to work if he could get out of it.

He didn't picture himself digging in the dirt; his silky coat might get dirty. And he couldn't see himself pulling weeds; some of the thorny weeds might poke him. But he still wanted a garden. He ordered some seed from the pretty picture seed catalog. When the seeds came, he found a place in the meadow that he thought would get a lot of sun, and he generously spread the seed that he had bought. Freddy then went home to await the harvest.

Gruff the Bear was never afraid of hard work or dirt. You would never say that Gruff's fur was silky. He knew from watching Farmer Brown that having a garden was more than just throwing out some seed. He got his whole family to join him, and they spent a lot of time digging up the soil, pulling out weeds, and spreading fertilizer. He read a book on gardening. When he got his seeds in the mail, he planted the rows just the right distance apart, and he put the seeds into the ground at just the right depth. He watered when it was dry and built a scarecrow to keep the birds away. Soon Gruff's hard work paid off, and he was selling fruit and vegetables at a stand on Ivy Lane right across from The Nut Hut.

When Freddy saw that Gruff was selling stuff at the Fruit and Vegetable Stand, he quickly went out to the place in the meadow where he had spread the seed. He not only couldn't find any vegetables, but he wasn't even sure of the exact place he had put the seeds. As Wise Old Owl saw Freddy looking for evidence of his seeds, he said, "It takes more than seeds to make a garden."

---

1. Attributed to Ezra Taft Benson on BrainyQuote, https://www.brainyquote.com/quotes/ezra_taft_benson_556124.

2. Attributed to Henry Ford on GoodReads, https://www.goodreads.com/quotes/37961-anyone-who-stops-learning-is-old-whether-at-twenty-or.

3. "You must be sure of two things: you must love your work, and not be always looking over the edge of it, wanting your play to begin. And the other is, you must not

be ashamed of your work, and think it would be more honorable to you to be doing something else. You must have a pride in your own work and in learning to do it well." George Eliot, *Middlemarch: A Study of Provincial Life*, vol. 2, Foleshill ed. (Boston: Little, Brown, and Company, 1900), 564.

4. Jason D. Stevens, "Vocation and the Apocalypse: McCarthy's *The Road*," Vocation Matters, August 14, 2019, https://vocationmatters.org/2019/08/14/apocalypse-mccarthys-the-road/

5. Ellen G. White, *Education* (Mountain View, CA: Pacific Press®, 1903), 17.

6. Albert J. Meyer, "The Church and Higher Education," Menno Simons Lectures, Monday, November 1, 1993.

7. Ellen G. White, *Special Testimonies on Education* (1897), 223.

8. Ellen G. White, *Manuscript Releases*, vol. 11 (Silver Spring, MD: Ellen G. White Estate, 1990), 170.

9. "The government of *Brave New World* retains control by making its citizens so happy and superficially fulfilled that they don't care about their personal freedom. In *Brave New World* the consequences of state control are a loss of dignity, morals, values, and emotions—in short, a loss of humanity." "Brave New World," SparkNotes, https://www.sparknotes.com/lit/bravenew/themes/.

Twelve

Sabbath

Experiencing and Living the Character of God

All of life senses time. Our hearts give us a sense of time and rhythm, and we feel secure in the regularity of events. The sun rises and sets with regularity. The moon provides months. The sun provides years. However, humans have not been satisfied with the biological sense of time and went about inventing clocks. At first, they were water clocks and sand glasses. Candles were also used to measure minutes, and by the seventeenth century, pendulum clocks measured seconds. The timekeeping pieces were all based on the length of the day, which is based on the rotation of the earth.

Today, we have an atomic clock that uses the cesium atom to measure time. It has 9,192,631,770 oscillations per second. The earth's rotation is no longer the standard to measure time. Every few years, a second is added to the year because the earth is slowing down, and time can be kept more accurately than the rotation of the earth. The cesium atomic clock is accurate to 1 second in 100 million years.[1]

We are in the century of the microsecond and the digital wristwatch. Our highly computerized society depends on hours, minutes, and seconds for its very existence. With news on the hour, work to the minute, and all timed to the second, we are slaves to the second hand. We know when we are late; we know when we are on time. We know when to go to work and when to get off work. We know the fastest mile run and the fastest quarter-mile time. We have divided, cut, split, and managed time. But somehow, we tend to lose the meaning of the life that we so accurately measure.

A taste of eternity

Have you ever felt with Shakespeare's Macbeth?

> Life's but a walking shadow, a poor player
> That struts and frets his hour upon the stage
> And then is heard no more: it is a tale
> Told by an idiot, full of sound and fury,
> Signifying nothing.[2]

Solomon felt like that. "I have seen all the things that are done under the sun; all of them are meaningless, a chasing after the wind" (Ecclesiastes 1:14). Have you ever felt you were just a position of the hands on the face of some eternal clock, ticking slowly to your end? Weeks come and go. Life ebbs away, and where did the time go?

Some might suggest that if they could only taste eternity, if they could only spend a moment there, they would be able to endure anything on this earth. Well, God gave us a gift so we could understand eternity. He gave us a taste of eternity. "By the seventh day God had finished the work he had been doing; so, on the seventh day he rested from all his work. And God blessed the seventh day and made it holy, because on it he rested from all the work of creating that he had done" (Genesis 2:2, 3).

To experience the Sabbath is to taste eternity. How is that taste to you? The Jews attempted to preserve their Sabbaths with many rules. Some Seventh-day Adventists, trying to preserve the Sabbath legalistically, use computers to determine the exact minute the sun sets. We know when the sun sets, we know when the Sabbath begins, and we memorize the fourth commandment. "Observe the Sabbath day, to keep it holy. Work six days and do everything you need to do. But the seventh day is a Sabbath to God, your God. Don't do any work—not you, nor your son, nor your daughter, nor your servant, nor your maid, nor your animals, not even the foreign guest visiting in your town. For in six days God made Heaven, Earth, and sea, and everything in them; he rested on the seventh day. Therefore, God blessed the Sabbath day; he set it apart as a holy day" (Exodus 20:8–11, *The Message*).

But with all our knowledge of the Sabbath, how much do we know about why it begins? Abraham Joshua Heschel, a famous Jewish author, wrote, "The meaning of the Sabbath is to celebrate time rather than space. Six days a week we live under the tyranny of things of space; on the Sabbath we try to become attuned to *holiness in time*. It is a day on which we are called upon to share in what is eternal in time, to turn from the results of creation to the mystery of creation; from the world of creation to the creation of the world."[3]

In our Sabbath Schools, what kind of education do we provide about the meaning of the Sabbath? A twenty-one-year-old has had three years of Sabbath time, and a seventy-year-old has spent ten years of life on Sabbath. What were those years like, those Sabbath years spent with Jesus? Have we been educated to love Jesus and experience a taste of eternity with Him? Or was it time spent waiting for the sun to set so we could do what we wanted? If we are anxious for Sabbath time to be over, will we be anxious for heaven to be over?

Sabbath enhances life

Time is life; life is time. Our lives and our time find meaning in the seventh of our time, of our life spent in God's presence on the Sabbath. The frustration we feel as life's seconds tick away can be answered during Sabbath time with Jesus. The message of the Sabbath is that you find meaning in life, not by measuring its events, your achievements, or your busy "doings" but by being in tune with God. Letting God fill your life instead of trying to fill it yourself with objects and self. The endless beat of life's directionless motion is answered in the Sabbath's statement that it is not what you do that gives you identity, but it is what you are that gives meaning to what you do. Heschel observes, "There is a realm of time where the goal is not to have but to be, not to own but to give, not to control but to share, not to subdue but to be in accord. Life goes wrong when the control of space, the acquisition of things of space, becomes our sole concern."[4]

The feeling of life's hurried meaninglessness is resolved in the Sabbath time of being God's child and not just a position of the hands on the face of an eternal clock that will soon tick us into unconsciousness. Sabbath is being in a relationship with the Lord of life. Can you keep the Sabbath without knowing Christ? Ellen White says, "In order to keep the Sabbath holy, men must themselves be holy."[5]

When our faith becomes a creed and our worship just a habit, when our church becomes a building rather than an instrument of service, when our religion is a series of doctrinal formulations rather than a way of compassionate living, then it is, as Shakespeare says, "a tale told by an idiot, full of sound and fury, signifying nothing."[6]

Anybody can clean the house on Friday and go to Sabbath School and church. Sabbath observance is a relationship with Jesus. If it is not that, it is not Sabbath observance.

"If you keep your feet from breaking the Sabbath
    and from doing as you please on my holy day,
if you call the Sabbath a delight
    and the LORD's holy day honorable,

and if you honor it by not going your own way
   and not doing as you please or speaking idle words,
then you will find your joy in the LORD,
   and I will cause you to ride on the heights of the land
   and to feast on the inheritance of your father Jacob."
   The mouth of the LORD has spoken (Isaiah 58:13, 14).

Sabbath is heaven on earth

When Jesus said, "The Sabbath was made for man, and not man for the Sabbath" (Mark 2:27, 28, NKJV), He was removing the burden that it had become and shining light on the purpose of the day. Seventh-day Adventists are concerned about future Sunday laws, when attempts will be made to take Sabbath observance away. How many of us love the Sabbath so much right now that we would be willing to die for it? A future Sunday law is not going to make us love the Sabbath. Christians are sealed not because they believe the seventh day is the Sabbath but because they have experienced Jesus on that day, letting nothing tear them away from Him and that experience.

Sabbath is like heaven, and heaven is not glorious because it has golden streets. Gold is precious because it is scarce; when it is not scarce, it will not be precious. Heaven is not glorious because of its beauty, though it will be beautiful. Heaven is not a place to go because you will not get sick there, though that will be nice.

What is the attraction of heaven? What is the attraction of the Sabbath? Heaven is glorious because our Lord will be there. Heaven derives its meaning from Jesus' presence. Sabbath is time spent in advance with that Person. Sabbath time is heaven on earth. Sabbath time is time to spend with Jesus. Being anxious to spend less time with Him is like declaring your love for a wife and not finding time in your schedule to be with her. Sabbath time gives meaning to all our lives, for Sabbath time brings us face-to-face with Him who made our lives and Him who justifies and sanctifies us. There is no meaning to life apart from Him who created it. There is no understanding of life apart from Him who gives us new life.

Time, all of time, is nothing than the measure of meaningless motions, the endless ticking of a cosmic clock, a walking shadow, waves disappearing on a pebbled shore. The lone exception to this rule is our relationship with our Creator, Jesus Christ. All of time, all of life without a relationship with Jesus, "is fleeting, / And our hearts, though stout and brave, / Still, like muffled drums, are beating / Funeral marches to the grave."[7]

Sabbath is a taste of eternity. What should I not do on the Sabbath? All that you do that destroys that relationship is Sabbath breaking. All that you do to enhance that relationship with Jesus is Sabbath keeping.

The Sabbath is a gift to be enjoyed

Once upon a time, there was a group of people who lived in the shadow of a large mountain. A wise king was the ruler of the people in the forest below the mountain. One day the kind king had to leave, but he told his people he would return, and when he returned, he would take them to the top of the mountain, where they would live forever. He would be gone for a long time, however, and so he told them that he was going to leave them a gift, a special gift so they would remember him while he was gone. When the wise king left the forest, he left in the center of it a beautiful fruit tree as his gift, telling them to protect the tree and enjoy the fruit of the tree until he returned.

At first, everyone happily protected and enjoyed the tree. They cut down all the weeds for some distance away and made sure it received a generous supply of water. The longer the king was gone, however, the more they thought of the tree and forgot the king. It was soon considered too sacred a tree for the birds to nest in, and it was protected from their nest-building activities. The tree was also fenced so that no bears could rub their backs against it. Many rules were developed concerning the care

116

of the tree. So intent were they on its preservation that no one ate the fruit of the tree; instead, they would take the fruit and preserve it in plastic. They sold the plasticized fruit as souvenirs. Many took the preserved fruit to their homes, where they placed it in special places to look at it. Only special people could sell and package the fruit, and the demand was very high. They forgot what the king was like. He appeared, as far as they were concerned, to be a harsh and demanding king because of all the rules they thought he had laid down about his tree.

The tree slowly gave less and less fruit, and no matter how hard the people worked, they could not get it to bear any better. Things got so bad that after several generations passed, they forgot the tree altogether. It was too much bother to care for it, and it had been so abused and commercialized by a few that they decided that they did not need it at all to remind them of the king. They had their plasticized fruit, and, after all, every tree could remind them of the king, and not just this one tree.

One day word went out that the king was coming back soon. Some remembered the king's gift, but they had a hard time finding it. The weeds had grown tall, and it was almost dead, save for a little bit of fruit that was still there. Carefully, those who had learned of the king's return nurtured the tree and gave it new life. At first, some of them would not eat of the tree because of the old traditions they remembered. But finally a few, remembering that it was a gift for them and for their good, decided to eat of it. The fruit was good. It was exhilarating. They were so excited about their tasting of the king's gift that they passed it around to as many as they could find who would sample it. They found that the tree, which had been producing very little fruit, began to produce abundantly. The more they gave away, the more it produced.

Excitedly, they ran through the community giving the fruit to others. They set up fruit stands all over the forest to get others to experience the king's gift. Some would not accept the fruit, and others were jealous of those who had found it. Some said they did not like it at all. But many ate of it and, in that experience, anticipated a time when the king, the giver of the gift, would return. Soon, as promised, the king did return and took everyone to the beautiful forest at the top of the great mountain. Everyone was excited, and when they arrived after the seven-day trip, they were very hungry. It was then that everyone discovered that the only food available there on the top of the mountain was the same kind of fruit as the gift that the king had given them in the other forest at the foot of the mountain.

All who enjoyed the fruit in the forest below loved the fruit on top of the mountain as well as the king who gave it to them. But some could not stand the taste of the fruit, and they asked to leave. Sorrowfully, the king complied with their request and allowed those who did not enjoy the fruit to leave. There was weeping and gnashing of teeth.

Sabbath time is a taste of eternity. A taste of time with Jesus. Do you enjoy the taste? Are you hungry for more?

---

1. Konstantin Bikos and Anne Buckle, "The Science Behind Leap Seconds," Timeanddate.com, accessed January 30, 2020, https://www.timeanddate.com/time /leap-seconds-background.html.

2. William Shakespeare, *Macbeth*, act 5, scene 5, http://shakespeare.mit.edu /macbeth/macbeth.5.5.html.

3. Abraham Joshua Heschel, *The Sabbath* (New York: Farrar, Straus and Giroux, 2005), 10.

4. Heschel, *The Sabbath*, 3.

5. Ellen G. White, *The Desire of Ages* (Mountain View, CA: Pacific Press®, 1940), 283.

6. Shakespeare, *Macbeth*, act 5, scene 5.

7. Henry Wadsworth Longfellow, "A Psalm of Life," Poetry Foundation, https:// www.poetryfoundation.org/poems/44644/a-psalm-of-life.

CHAPTER
Thirteen

Heaven, Education, and Eternal Learning

In *The Adventures of Huckleberry Finn*, the Christian spinster Miss Watson takes a dim view of Huck's fun-loving spirit and describes a heaven that is not exciting to Huck. "She went on and told me all about the good place. She said all a body would have to do there was to go around all day long with a harp and sing, forever and ever. So I didn't think much of it. . . . I asked her if she reckoned Tom Sawyer would go there, and she said not by a considerable sight. I was glad about that, because I wanted him and me to be together."[1]

What is heaven like?
Many are the different perspectives on what happens when you die, but in general, there is agreement on one thing: when you die, something happens. Randy Alcorn, in his book on heaven, says,

The sense that we will live forever *somewhere* has shaped every civilization in human history. Australian aborigines pictured Heaven as a distant island beyond the western horizon. The early Finns thought it was an island in the faraway east. Mexicans, Peruvians, and Polynesians believed that they went to the sun or the moon after death. Native Americans believed that in the afterlife their spirits would hunt the spirits of buffalo. The *Gilgamesh* epic, an ancient Babylonian legend, refers to a resting place of heroes and hints at a tree of life. In the pyramids of Egypt, the embalmed bodies had maps placed beside them as guides to the future world. The Romans believed that the righteous would picnic in the Elysian fields while their horses grazed nearby. . . . Although these depictions of the afterlife differ, the unifying testimony of the human heart throughout history is belief in life after death. Anthropological evidence suggests that every culture has a God-given, innate sense of the eternal—that this world is not all there is.[2]

When I think of heaven, I usually see swans on lakes, lots of green, white puffy clouds, and people robed in white. I think I am seeing pictures I saw as a child from the Bible storybooks. One thing is certain: Jesus taught that there was such a place and that He is preparing for us to be there (see John 14:1–3).

What kind of existence will we have in heaven? We live in a three-dimensional world. Is there another dimension—say, a fourth dimension? If you were in the fourth dimension, could you move to the third but not be seen by those in the third dimension? Is that where angels exist? "The mathematics used in superstring theory requires at least 10 dimensions."[3] Albert Einstein speculated about the possibility of the existence of a parallel universe. If we could travel through a black hole, would we arrive in heaven? There is so much we don't understand about the universe!

What will heaven be like? For me, heaven raises many questions. We talk about it and long for it, but what is it that we long for? Is heaven a fancy retirement center with golden streets? Is heaven where all our needs are cared for, like a retirement village in Florida?

Gary Larson captured a common misperception of heaven in one of his Far Side cartoons. In it, a man with angel wings and halo sits on a cloud doing nothing, with no one nearby. He has the expression of someone marooned on a desert island with absolutely nothing to do. A caption shows his inner thoughts: "Wish I'd brought a magazine."

When the Sadducees, who did not believe in the resurrection or heaven, asked Jesus who the spouse of the woman would be who was married seven times, Jesus replied, "At the resurrection people will neither marry nor be given in marriage; they will be like the angels in heaven" (Matthew 22:30).

That text bothered me until my wife and I agreed that we might not be married in heaven, but we would live together anyway. Jesus says we will be like the angels, but what are angels like? Are they immaterial? Are they just spirits? Can they pass through to other dimensions? I have a hard time imagining personality and personhood without materiality, without a body. Questions like this sparked debate in the Middle Ages about how many angels could dance on the head of a pin.

Heaven is real

The Bible's descriptions of heaven indicate that it is a physical place. We read in Isaiah, "They will build houses and dwell in them; they will plant vineyards and eat their fruit" (Isaiah 65:21). And,

> "the wolf and the lamb will feed together,
>   and the lion will eat straw like the ox,
> They will neither harm nor destroy in all my holy mountain,"
>   says the LORD (verse 25).

The Lord is communicating to the tribes of Israel who were building houses that were occupied by others, planting vineyards that the Philistines would harvest, and protecting flocks from wolves and lions. Maybe Isaiah's point is to picture a place of safety and security rather than seeking to describe the dietary habits of lions in heaven.

The Bible indicates that things will be enough the same that we will recognize each other: "Now we see but a poor reflection as in a mirror; then we shall see face to face. Now I know in part; then I shall know fully, even as I am fully known" (1 Corinthians 13:12). This reality is called the new earth. It is not called the new spirit world or the new ghost town. John gives us a taste of heaven in Revelation 21, where he describes the New Jerusalem with jewels and golden streets. It reminds me of the man who went to heaven with a big suitcase, and when Saint Peter told him he was not allowed to bring anything into heaven, the man pleaded otherwise. So finally Saint Peter said to him, "OK, let me see what you have in the suitcase." The man opened it up, and it was filled with bars of gold. Saint Peter said, "I see you are bringing street pavers."

The biblical descriptions of heaven are more meaningful than shiny jewels and gold streets. Gold is precious because it is rare. If you use it like asphalt, it is not particularly valuable. The biblical descriptions are symbolic. It is a safe place; lions eat straw and lie down with the calves. It is a protected place; the walls of the city are huge. It is a beautiful place; the streets are made of gold, and the gates are pearls. But most of all, it is a place Jesus has prepared for us, and Ellen White describes its importance: "No voices of contention mar the sweet and perfect peace of heaven. . . . All is in perfect harmony, in perfect order and perfect bliss. . . . Love reigns there. There are no jarring elements, no discord or contentions or war of words."[4]

Enjoying heaven
A swan alighted by the banks of the pond in which a crane was wading, seeking snails.

"Where did you come from?" asked the crane.

"I came from heaven," replied the swan.

"And where is heaven?" asked the crane.

The swan then described the glories of heaven with streets of gold, precious stones, and a tree of life.

The crane showed no interest and finally asked, "Will there be any snails there?"

"Of course not," replied the swan.

"Then," said the crane as he continued his search for snails, "you can have your heaven; I want snails."[5]

If we think of heaven in terms of, *I get to do what I enjoy. I get to fly here or there. I can sleep in till noon and will have angels at my beck and call.* If we think of heaven in terms of, *I do not have to do this anymore.* Or, *I will not have to go to work, or clean the house, or do anything I do not want to.* If our focus is on how heaven will be for our eternal pleasure, fulfilling our needs, satisfying our desires, and getting it all, all we ever wanted and more, then heaven would be boring, because as finite beings, we could not survive infinity focused on ourselves. It would eventually prove boring and devolve into hell. The unselfish environment of heaven would be unbearable for a selfish person.

Pleasure sought for self is, in the end, destructive. Heaven is not a solution to selfishness, filling our every want. Hell is the ultimate solution to selfishness. Heaven is a place for those who have learned selflessness, for only the selfless can enjoy eternal existence. Heaven is not an eternal Disney World where our longings are filled with ever longer rides on Magic Mountain. The only way finite creatures can enjoy infinite time is to be focused outside of self. When I am unselfishly focused on others and Jesus, there is an eternity of joy to explore. Heaven is an eternal school where we will not only be taught but also teach others about our experiences of life on earth. Along with unfallen beings, we will be giving of ourselves to others. Ellen White says, "In heaven none will think of self, nor seek their own pleasure; but all, from pure genuine love, will seek the happiness of the heavenly beings around them. If we wish to enjoy heavenly society in the earth made new, we must be governed by heavenly principles here."[6]

Imagining heaven

Given our limited capacity to understand the universe and our limited understanding of heaven, we can identify with Paul, who wrote,

"No eye has seen,
 no ear has heard,
no mind has conceived
  what God has prepared for those who love him" (1 Corinthians 2:9).

Is it totally incomprehensible? Most people stop after reading verse 9, essentially saying that it is futile to consider the prospect, yet Paul continues, "but God has revealed it to us by his Spirit" (verse 10).

What has God revealed? Ellen White saw heaven and wrote, "Language is altogether too feeble to attempt a description of heaven. As the scene rises before me, I am lost in amazement. Carried away with the surpassing splendor and excellent glory, I lay down the pen and exclaim, 'Oh, what love! what wondrous love!' The most exalted language fails to describe the glory of heaven or the matchless depths of a Saviour's love."[7]

What stands out in Ellen White's description? It is the love of Jesus, not physical beauty. She joins Paul in saying you cannot describe it. Heaven is the fulfillment of innermost longings, scratching where we don't even know we itch. It is to be fully known. To feel like I fit in, like I really belong. C. S. Lewis says, "There have been times . . . when I think we do not desire heaven but more often I find myself wondering whether, in our heart of hearts, we have ever desired anything else."[8]

In Lewis's *The Lion, the Witch, and the Wardrobe*, Edmund seeks to fill the "God-shaped vacuum" with Turkish delight. There is a God-shaped void in all of humankind. Many today seek to fill it with addictions, gadgets, and workaholism, but it cannot be filled by any created thing.

When I attended the seminary in Michigan, I planned for weeks and months to go back to California for Christmas vacation. It was not to see California, not to see orange trees, and not to bask in the sunshine. I was eager to see a person. I was eager to see Cynthia, my future wife. Heaven is about being with our Savior. Heaven is about being with our Creator. The glory of heaven is "the matchless depths of a Saviour's love."[9]

Blaise Pascal is paraphrased as saying, "There is a God-shaped *vacuum* in the heart of every person which cannot be filled by *any* created thing, but only by *God*."[10] Have you ever put together a puzzle with a group of friends at Christmas or Thanksgiving? Everyone works hard, and slowly, from the edges, the puzzle takes shape. There are cries of success as pieces are found and put into place. There are complaints about the difficulty of the puzzle, and people search for a piece they cannot find.

Eventually, the work nears completion, and with great excitement, the last few pieces are put into place. The work goes faster and faster, but in the end, one piece remains elusive. It seems to be missing. There is a hole in the picture. It is not complete. Everyone searches, under the sofa, under the table, under chairs. Finally, with a shout of joy someone says, "I found it!" Everyone struggles to have a hand in putting in the last piece to complete the puzzle, and finally, the picture is complete.

The person who knows us the best does not really know us. The person who likes us the most does not like us totally. The person who enjoys us the most does not always enjoy us. Even when we feel at home, we are never completely at home. Heaven, however, is designed for us. There is a missing piece in the heavenly puzzle that we were intended to fill. There is a void in the heart of our Creator that we were shaped for. We will fit. We will be fully known. We will finally be at home with Jesus, our Creator.

The message we need to learn about heaven is the message we need to live on earth. Ellen White describes it like this: "The great controversy is ended. Sin and sinners are no more. The entire universe is clean. One pulse of harmony and gladness beats through the vast creation. From Him who created all, flow life and light and gladness, throughout the realms of illimitable space. From the minutest atom to the greatest world, all things, animate and inanimate, in their unshadowed beauty and perfect joy, declare that God is love."[11]

Fenton Forest

Once upon a time in Fenton Forest, Gruff the Bear was being his usual self, complaining about everything. He never did find much that was pleasant about anything in the forest. But it seemed that this time, his complaining was worse than usual.

"Nobody ever does anything for anyone in this place!" Gruff complained. "Scamper the Squirrel keeps all his nuts for himself, and the bees don't want to share their honey with me. Everybody always just looks out for number one. I long for that day when I can move to Friendly Forest."

Now Friendly Forest, in forest folklore, was where all good members of the forest family went when they died. (At one time it was called the happy hunting ground, but that didn't sound good to several forest folk for obvious reasons.)

When Freddy the Fox heard Gruff say that he could hardly wait to go to Friendly Forest, he told him that he would oblige him by pushing him over the cliff by Crashing Creek, but Gruff didn't think that was funny. Gruff went on and on about how wonderful it would be to live in Friendly Forest:

- There would be berries to eat without having to crawl through the briars to get them.
- There would be a constant supply of honey, for the bees would be generous, providing him with all he could eat.
- There would be a lot of trout, and they would jump out of the river onto the bank whenever he was hungry.
- There would always be a bright sun to warm his full stomach.
- And most of all, as far as Gruff was concerned, Freddy the Fox wouldn't be there, so that would make it a truly friendly forest.

In the past, forest folk tolerated Gruff's constant complaining, but this time it was getting on their nerves. One day, Wise Old Owl met Gruff along Crooked Path and said to him, "Gruff, you complain so much, as soon as you arrive in Friendly Forest, it will no longer be friendly."

"Everyone will be so nice there, I would have no reason to complain," said Gruff.

"Not so," said Wise Old Owl. "They change their location but not their disposition, those who move to Friendly Forest."

---

1. Mark Twain, *The Adventures of Huckleberry Finn* (n.p.: Grosset & Dunlap, 1918), 3, 4.

2. Randy Alcorn, *Heaven* (n.p.: Tyndale, 2004), xix.

3. Rick Groleau, "Imagining Other Dimensions," NOVA, July 2003, http://www.pbs.org/wgbh/nova/elegant/dimensions.html.

4. Arthur White, *The Lonely Years: 1876–1891*, vol. 3 of the Ellen G. White Biography (Washington, DC: Review and Herald*, 1984), 202.

5. Stanley I. Stuber and Thomas Curtis Clark, *Treasury of the Christian Faith: An Encyclopedic Handbook of the Range and Witness of Christianity* (New York: Association Press, 1949), 355.

6. Ellen G. White, *Testimonies for the Church*, vol. 2 (Mountain View, CA: Pacific Press*, 1948), 132, 133.

7. Ellen G. White, *The Adventist Home* (Nashville, TN: Southern Publishing, 1952), 538.

8. Wayne Martindale, *Beyond the Shadowlands: C. S. Lewis on Heaven and Hell* (Wheaton, IL: Crossway Books, 2005), 16.

9. White, *Adventist Home*, 538.

10. "Blaise Pascal Quotes," GoodReads, https://www.goodreads.com/quotes /801132-there-is-a-god-shaped-vacuum-in-the-heart-of-each; emphasis added.

11. Ellen G. White, *The Great Controversy Between Christ and Satan* (Mountain View, CA: Pacific Press®, 1950), 678.